LOVE
and TERROR
in the GOD
ENCOUNTER

Other Books by David Hartman

Epistles of Maimonides:
Crisis and Leadership
(Jewish Publication Society)

The Breakdown of Tradition and the Quest for Renewal:
Reflections on Three Jewish Responses to Modernity
(Gate Press)

Conflicting Visions:
Spiritual Possibilities of Modern Israel
(Schocken Books)

A Heart of Many Rooms:
Celebrating the Many Voices within Judaism
(Jewish Lights Publishing)

Israelis and the Jewish Tradition:
An Ancient People Debating Its Future
(Yale University Press)

Joy and Responsibility:
Israel, Modernity and the Renewal of Judaism
(Ben Zvi-Pozner)

A Living Covenant:
The Innovative Spirit in Traditional Judaism
(Jewish Lights Publishing)

Maimonides:
Torah and the Philosophic Quest
with Shlomo Pines
(Jewish Publication Society)

LOVE
and TERROR
in the GOD
ENCOUNTER

The Theological Legacy of
Rabbi Joseph B. Soloveitchik

DAVID HARTMAN

JEWISH LIGHTS Publishing
Woodstock, Vermont

Love and Terror in the God Encounter:
The Theological Legacy of Rabbi Joseph B. Soloveitchik

2004 First Quality Paperback Printing
2001 First Hardcover Printing
© 2001 by David Hartman

Library of Congress Cataloging-in-Publication Data

Hartman, David, 1931–
Love and Terror in the God Encounter: The Theological Legacy of Rabbi Joseph B. Soloveitchik / David Hartman.
p.   cm.
Includes bibliographical references and index.
ISBN 1-58023-112-8 (hardcover)
1. Soloveitchik, Joseph Dov—Teachings. 2. Jewish way of life. 3. Judaism—Doctrines. 4. Jewish law—Philosophy. 5. Faith (Judaism). 6. Prayer—Judaism. I. Title.
BM755.S593 H37 2001
296.8'32'092—dc21

                                                          2001000882

ISBN 1-58023-176-4 (paperback)

10 9 8 7 6 5 4 3 2 1

Manufactured in the United States of America

Published by Jewish Lights Publishing
A Division of LongHill Partners, Inc.
Sunset Farm Offices, Route 4, P.O. Box 237
Woodstock, VT 05091
Tel: (802) 457-4000   Fax: (802) 457-4004
www.jewishlights.com

To our children,

Dvorah, Tova, Moishe, Donniel, Adina,
Adina, Aren, Ranan & Maya

This book was generated as part of the ongoing research of the
Richard and Sylvia Kaufman Center for
Contemporary Jewish Thought at the
Shalom Hartman Institute in Jerusalem.

The Center explores and encourages new spiritual possibilities
emerging from the confrontation of the Judaic tradition with
modernity. The Shalom Hartman Institute, founded in 1976,
is an advanced research and teacher-training center whose
mission is to meet the new intellectual and spiritual
challenges facing the Jewish people resulting from both the
rebirth of Israel and the full participation of
modern Jews in Western culture.

CONTENTS

PREFACE   ix

1. INTRODUCTION   1

2. THE HALAKHIC HERO   23

3. THE RELIGIOUS PASSION OF HALAKHIC MAN   63

4. THE LONELY MAN OF FAITH   97

5. CONFRONTATION   131

6. PRAYER   167

BIBLIOGRAPHY   213

INDEX   215

PREFACE

As a young person my education was mediated by talmudic masters of the Eastern European tradition. I vividly recall the experience of being exposed to, for the first time, a great talmudic master who delivered a theology lecture on prayer in which the ideas of Søren Kierkegaard and Rudolph Otto played a central role. Suddenly, like a cool, refreshing breeze, a new religious phenomenology became alive to me. From that moment on, my orientation to Judaism was forever altered. That teacher who changed the direction of my intellectual life was Rabbi Joseph B. Soloveitchik, of blessed memory.

I cannot sufficiently articulate the profound influence that R. Soloveitchik had on my study of talmudic texts, my religious thinking, and my whole understanding of Judaism. I recall writing to him and saying, "You were responsible for my moving into philosophical studies." It was he, in fact, who wrote my letter of recommendation to Fordham University's graduate school.

In the course of my philosophical studies and at crucial

moments in my life when I experienced difficult periods of doubt and questioned some of the prevailing, widely accepted theological and moral positions found in the halakhic tradition, he was the figure, the living image that nurtured and sustained my commitment. His impact on me during my ten years of studying with him has never lost its power and influence.

R. Soloveitchik represented a Judaism committed to intellectual courage, integrity, and openness—the antithesis to dogmatism and fanaticism. Ideas never frightened him. I never once heard him say, "*Apikorsis!* This is heretical! You should not think such thoughts or consider such ideas!" Nothing intimidated him intellectually. He believed in and communicated to his students the freedom to engage the philosophical, theological, and cultural traditions of Western civilization.

Through R. Soloveitchik's example, I went on to develop my own approach to talmudic studies and philosophy of Halakhah. My loyalty to and love for him as my teacher never interfered with my own intellectual independence and critical appreciation of his writings.

R. Soloveitchik exemplified how respect and reverence for the talmudic and philosophical giants of the tradition are not incompatible with taking issue intellectually with their views or interpretations. He had a profound impatience and disdain for intellectual timidity. I offer this volume, which reflects my lifelong engagement with his writings, as the tribute of a grateful student to his beloved teacher.

This book, which is the first of two volumes, does not address all of R. Soloveitchik's theological essays. The present volume focuses mainly on the essays "Ish ha-Halakhah" ("Halakhic Man"), "Lonely Man of Faith," "Confrontation," and various writings on prayer. The second volume will address specific themes such as *teshuvah,* history, and R. Soloveitchik's approach to religious Zionism.

This work has benefited from discussions with my colleagues at the Robert and Arlene Kogod Institute for Advanced Judaic Studies of the Shalom Hartman Institute. I am grateful to my research associate and student Elliott Yagod for his assistance in bringing this work to fruition—his patience, devotion, and clarity of thought have made my work possible; to Professors Gerald Blidstein, William Kolbrener, Yehudah Gellman, and Steven Kepnes for their critical responses and suggestions; to Ruth Sherer, my devoted secretary, who conscientiously and patiently worked on my many revisions; and to my publisher Stuart Matlins, editor Elisheva Urbas, and to Sandra Korinchak and the staff at Jewish Lights. It has been a distinct pleasure for me to be involved with a publisher so dedicated to disseminating a writer's work to as many people as possible.

It is my fervent hope that this work will contribute to an in-depth discussion of the writings of R. Soloveitchik and to a renewed reading of his work with a sympathetic yet critical eye. This is the legacy he left to me and to all who are prepared to grapple with the subtlety and complexity of his theological and midrashic thought.

I dedicate this volume to my loving children, who patiently listened to and contributed to their father's lifelong intellectual struggle with Rabbi Soloveitchik's theological legacy.

INTRODUCTION

THE RESURGENCE OF ORTHODOXY

One of the most remarkable and unanticipated features of Jewish life in the post-Holocaust period has been the resurgence of the Eastern European style of Orthodox Judaism, especially in Israel and North America. In the 1940s and 1950s people spoke of the impending demise of Orthodoxy. The North American Jewish communities were moving toward Conservative and Reform; Israel presented an image of anticlerical socialist Jewish nationalism. Many predicted the eventual disappearance of Orthodoxy and the triumph of modernity and secularism throughout the Jewish world. To be an Orthodox rabbi in America at that time was to feel oneself in a defensive posture, and to find one's synagogue membership predominantly drawn from the older generation. If religious institutional affiliation is a form of social identification, then people preferred the "crowd" that gathered at Conservative or Reform congregations.

In Israel, secular Zionism was triumphant. The religious Zionist community fought defensive battles to protect their educational institutions. Clearly, the Jewish people were moving away from tradition, abandoning the old patterns of daily life organized around the normative structure of Torah and Halakhah.

Sociologists were writing about the end of traditional society. The world of the yeshivah, of intense Torah learning and of the all-enveloping framework of the Halakhah, was on the verge of collapse. A new secular Jew was emerging. The views of medieval theologians such as Saadiah Gaon and Maimonides, for whom Torah was constitutive of Jewish identity, were losing all relevance. The Sinai covenant and halakhic practice were viewed as instrumental values that had served to maintain the Jewish people throughout their exilic history but were replaced by the spirit of nationalism that had brought about the rebirth of the modern State of Israel.

In Israel, Jewish life was being organized by new instruments, such as the Hebrew language, the commitment to Jewish continuity and to the flourishing of the Jewish state in Israel, the pioneering spirit required to resettle the land, army service, and so on. A cultural revolution of the highest order was succeeding. The image of the Jew as the student of Torah in the *beit midrash*, the rabbinic house of study, was overshadowed by the tanned, heroic pioneer, who saw, in the building of the land and in the establishment of strong defense forces, new outlets for a passionate commitment to Jewish history.

As a symbolic gesture toward a waning traditional culture, the Israeli government was prepared to excuse Orthodox yeshivah students from army service. Allowing this small flame of Torah to continue burning in the small town of Bnei Brak or in certain sections of Jerusalem was tantamount to lighting a memorial lamp for the culture destroyed in the Holocaust.

This, then, was the apparent situation of Judaism in the mid-twentieth century, both in the Diaspora and in Israel. Hitler had given the final deathblow to a two-thousand-year-old talmudic civilization that had already been undermined and severely weakened by the spirit of modernity and secularism. A new Jewish people shaped by modern values was now emerging. Jews were preparing to recite the final *kaddish* (mourner's prayer) for the death of this ancient, once vital, but never-to-be-resurrected halakhic civilization.

Since then, this seemingly inevitable secularization process has undergone a sharp reversal. In Israel, North America, and throughout the world, the group within the Jewish people that exudes the most vitality, self-confidence, and numerical growth is right-wing Orthodoxy. They are filled with enthusiasm and self-confidence in their ability to shape the future character of the Jewish people. One of the manifest characteristics of the right-wing Orthodox camp is its absolute refusal to compromise with modern values, such as equality of the sexes, religious pluralism, and universal human rights. The traditional gender roles within the Jewish family and community are affirmed as strongly as ever. The birthrate among this group is extremely high. Many Eastern European yeshivot decimated by the Nazis have been rebuilt into even larger institutions. Never before in Jewish history have so many Jews been engaged in talmudic study as in Israel today. The leadership of the right-wing Orthodox community is drawn from the academies of Jewish talmudic learning where leadership is determined by mastery and allegiance to the talmudic tradition. They are the current role models and mediators of the Jewish heritage. When a great sage died recently, over two hundred thousand people followed his bier through the streets of Jerusalem.

Torah-observant communities, bustling families, and powerful educational institutions are emerging with enormous vigor. The Israeli government no longer views non-Zionist religious parties as flickering memorial candles about to be extinguished, but as powerful pressure groups holding the balance of power between the two major political blocs. The future of the Zionist state is thus being significantly influenced by non-Zionist elements. I use the term "non-Zionist" because this community does not see any religious significance in the national rebirth of Israel, nor does it see the political state as having any significance for the future of Judaism. While regarding cooperation with and participation in the government as permissible, they do so only to protect their own educational institutions and the welfare of their burgeoning population. They do not religiously celebrate Israel's Independence Day, nor do they see any value or moral need to serve in the Israel Defense Forces. They conceive of the Jewish people as a Torah people meant to establish its national political existence under a messianic king whose knowledge of Torah and allegiance to its commandments are preconditions for Jewish political leadership.

This community is so confident of its ultimate victory that it allows itself to manifest an aggressive posture to all groups that it views as deviating from the normative tradition of Judaism. There is no cooperation at all with Conservative, Reform, or Reconstructionist rabbis. Orthodox rabbis are prohibited from joining rabbinic bodies in which non-Orthodox rabbis are members. Clear barriers prevent any social and religious contacts between traditional Orthodoxy and those groups that are accused of having "compromised" the tradition for the sake of modernity. Accordingly, pressure is exerted in Israel to delegitimize the Conservative and Reform rabbinates. Conversions to Judaism conducted by non-Orthodox rabbis are rejected. The Orthodox parties pressure the Knesset to pass legislation excluding people converted by Conservative or Reform religious courts from claiming the right to Israeli citizenship under the Law of Return. Marriages and divorces performed by Conservative or Reform rabbis have been delegitimized. Negotiations over these issues regularly precede the formation of coalition governments in Israel. The first Likud-led government came about after its predecessor fell following a dispute about a violation of the Sabbath.

4

The single-minded dedication of this Orthodox orientation to an insulated, ghettolike religious education, the emphasis upon large families, the meticulous commitment to halakhic observance, and the repudiation of Western humanistic values have proven successful in resurrecting the Eastern European form of Jewish life. We are experiencing today a powerful revival of a form of Judaism that totally repudiates any attempt to integrate the Jewish tradition with modernity. Whether modernity takes the intellectual form of study of Western literature and philosophy or the nationalist form of the Zionist revolution and the establishment of the State of Israel, the repudiation is equally emphatic.

THE REVISIONIST INTERPRETATION OF R. SOLOVEITCHIK

In the light of the emerging strength and vitality of this form of Jewish life, the figure of Rabbi Joseph B. Soloveitchik, of blessed memory, towers above all other modern Jewish religious thinkers. The future of both religious Zionism in Israel and of Orthodoxy in America hangs to a great extent on how we interpret R. Soloveitchik's intellectual legacy. R. Soloveitchik was the leading Orthodox talmudic scholar and theologian in North America for over half a century. Thousands of his students at Yeshiva University shaped what became identified as "modern Orthodoxy." Whenever the question was raised whether a shared universe of discourse is possible between the tradition of Torah study and Western philosophical thought, the standard answer at Yeshiva University was to point to the example of "the Rav." Here was an individual who captivated his students equally by his brilliant skills in talmudic dialectics and by his profound knowledge of modern theology. R. Soloveitchik bore witness to the legitimacy of remaining loyal to the Judaic tradition without sacrificing one's intellectual freedom and honesty.

Students of R. Soloveitchik did not experience the tradition as culturally fragile or as incapable of intellectually engaging contemporary theologians and philosophers. I personally cannot forget the feeling of intellectual stimulation and liberation I felt when I went from the traditional Lakewood yeshivah to study with R. Soloveitchik. Nothing in the Western intellectual tradition was considered *"treif"* or dangerous. I felt encouraged to think independently and critically about my own tradition and to roam freely and to feel at home in the broader context of the Western intellectual tradition.

From the extensive footnotes in all of R. Soloveitchik's writings, it is obvious that the thinkers who shaped his appreciation of life and set his intellectual agenda were not exclusively from the rabbinic tradition. In this sense, his attitude to philosophy corresponds in a significant way to what Prof. Shlomo Pines wrote about Maimonides.

> The fact that, relatively speaking, Maimonides had so little recourse to Jewish philosophic literature is significant. It implies inter alia that he had no use for a specific Jewish philosophic tradition. In spite of the convenient fiction, which he repeats, that the philosophic sciences flourished among the Jews of antiquity, he evidently considered that philosophy transcended religious or national distinction.[1]

In spite of the obvious significance of R. Soloveitchik for modern Judaism, during the last several years a major attempt has emerged to present and interpret him as a traditional *rosh yeshivah* (talmudic teacher and leader in the Eastern European mode). Many now argue that R. Soloveitchik never intended to bring any

---

[1]Shlomo Pines, "Translator's Introduction," in Moses Maimonides, *The Guide for the Perplexed,* trans. Shlomo Pines (Chicago and London: Univ. of Chicago Press, 1963), cxxiii–cxxi.

new, radically innovative intellectual perspectives to traditional Judaism. While they admit that he used and was engaged in modern existentialist thought, they claim that R. Soloveitchik's sole purpose was apologetic, that is, to strengthen the claim of Halakhah on the modern Jew. His brother, Rabbi Aaron Soloveitchik, wrote that he used the Western intellectual tradition to attract and to influence college-educated Jews. His use of Western philosophy was an external trapping that did not reflect his true traditional religious soul, which should be understood in terms of the same traditional piety exemplified by his father and his grandfather. Fundamentally, according to this argument, R. Soloveitchik must be understood within the same parameters with which we understand the Lithuanian talmudic giants that emerged in Eastern Europe.

The fact that in all of his vast intellectual output there are no significantly new, bold halakhic guidelines lends support to the claim that R. Soloveitchik must be understood within the classical tradition of Orthodoxy. His halakhic *hiddushim* (innovations) are not markedly different from those of traditional rabbis. It was possible to study a variety of talmudic tractates with him without sensing that this brilliant talmudist was also the author of innovative theological essays. In particular, he wrote no major responsa reflecting susceptibility to modern concerns and sensibilities. Indeed, one would be hard-pressed to find anything in his strictly halakhic writings or discussions remotely comparable in originality or daring to his work on Judaic religious phenomenology and theology.

Since R. Soloveitchik himself claimed that all authentic Jewish thought must be grounded in halakhic norms, his disinclination to engage the modern world on the concrete level of halakhic decision-making raises serious doubts about his supposed modernism. How can one say that R. Soloveitchik was seriously engaged by modern values if they are not reflected in his halakhic thinking? He may have made philosophical excursions to Athens, Berlin, and New York. One reads about his being engaged by the ideas of Plato, Aristotle, Herman Cohen, Kant, and William James. There is no doubt that he flew all around the contemporary intellectual map, but ultimately he always landed firmly back at his traditional spiritual home of Brisk.

At the beginning of his adventure with Western philosophy, one might have thought that there would be important surprises in store for twentieth-century Orthodox Judaism. Nevertheless, traditionalists in the Orthodox camp feel assured that in spite of all the bright modern colors in R. Soloveitchik's theological sketches, everything remains the same and nothing in the tradition needs to be rethought or redirected. In the following chapters, I will argue that this revisionist reading of R. Soloveitchik is misguided. With all his concern to underpin the Orthodox tradition, there is something radically new in his understanding of "halakhic man." R. Soloveitchik is a complex figure. He is indeed firmly rooted in his family's halakhic tradition, yet he is also genuinely responsive to modern Western theology. Although he always remained committed to perpetuating his father's halakhic legacy, he also labored to define an ideal halakhic type of person who embodies the modern values of individuality, creativity, and autonomy.

To appreciate R. Soloveitchik's innovative contribution to modern Judaism, it is essential that we first take note of some of the typical sensibilities of the traditional halakhic personality. In particular, we will consider the important strand in Orthodox Judaism that nurtured a ghetto mentality, repudiating alien thought and values. This spirit of insulation grew through a development of halakhic practice and learning that claimed to be intellectually and morally self-sufficient.

THE SELF-SUFFICIENCY OF
HALAKHIC JUDAISM

In the biblical story of the Exodus and of Israel's sojourn in the desert, God is portrayed as actively involved in the historical and daily life of the community. God defeats pharaoh in an open, dramatic struggle visible to all: "And the Egyptians shall know that I am the Lord, when I stretch out my hand over Egypt and bring out the Israelites from their midst" (Exod. 7:5).

In the Exodus drama, it is made obvious to the Egyptians who is the Lord of History. Both the manner of the Sinai revelation and the sustaining concern of God throughout the difficult trek in the desert testify to a God who is active and visible in the community's life. When enemies such as Amalek seek Israel's defeat, Moses is informed how God will bring victory to his people. The powerful Lord of History elects Israel as God's chosen people. All who wish to defeat Israel are made aware of God's protective concern for this community. In return for God's protection, Israel must promise exclusive allegiance to their almighty divine King.

Faith in God and the obligation to obey God's commandments are based upon the visible manifestation of God's triumphant liberating power.

> *I am the Lord thy God.* Why were the Ten Commandments not said at the beginning of the Torah? They give a parable. To what may this be compared? To the following: A king who entered a province said to the people: May I be your king? But the people said to him: Have you done anything good for us that you should rule over us? What did he do then? He built the city wall for them, he brought in the water supply for them, and he fought their battles. Then when he said to them: May I be your king? They said to him: Yes, yes. Likewise,

9

God. He brought the Israelites out of Egypt, divided the sea for them, sent down the manna for them, brought up the well for them, brought the quails for them. He fought for them the battle with Amalek. Then he said to them: I am to be your king. And they said to Him: Yes, yes. (*Mek. Bahodesh Exod.* 20.2)

This image of the visible, triumphant Lord of History had to be rethought as a result of the destruction of the Second Temple and the loss of political sovereignty. How does a community sustain loyalty to God under political conditions that suggest a defeated rather than a victorious God? How do you make God's presence and Torah to be seen as a living reality when the ongoing direct involvement of God in history is no longer evident? What is Israel to believe when the nations of the world no longer tremble at God's providential and particular love for Israel? Where is the living word of God when prophets no longer hear God's speech?

The following midrash captures one way in which rabbinic Judaism rethought its biblical foundations. It redefined the meaning of divine power in the light of Israel's political weakness and humiliation.

Why were they called men of the Great Assembly? Because they restored the crown of the divine attributes to its ancient completeness. Moses had come and said: "the great, the mighty, and the awesome God" [Deut. 10:17]. Then Jeremiah came and said: "Aliens are frolicking in His temple; where then are His awesome deeds?" Hence he omitted the word "awesome" [in Jer. 32:18]. Daniel came and said: "Aliens are enslaving His sons; where are His mighty deeds?" Hence he omitted the word "mighty" [in Dan. 9:4]. But they came and said: "On the contrary! Therein lie His mighty deeds that He suppresses His wrath, that He extends long-suffering to the wicked. Therein lie His awesome powers: For but for fear of Him, how could one [single] nation persist among the [many] nations?" (b. *Yoma* 69b)

The victorious warrior God in the story of the liberation from Egypt becomes the silent long-suffering God whose power is not expressed in the quick defeat of Israel's enemies. The vision of history in which all nations were meant to proclaim "the Lord of Israel is King" must be suppressed and postponed. New forms had to be found to express the vitality and presence of God in the community. A way was needed to make God's relational presence felt in the community despite political weakness and vulnerability. The theological connotations of political power, which is central to the history of all nations, had to be neutralized; Israel had to be given a new way of understanding the glory of God's kingdom and the Jewish people's role in history.

The rabbinic institution of prayer dramatically rehearsed the larger picture of God's intimate connection with Israel's historical destiny. The liturgy reinforced the belief that eventually Israel will be vindicated for its faithful waiting. The suffering servant, Israel, will shine forth in full glory when God becomes king over all of humanity. The world will one day see Israel no longer despised among the nations, but restored as the mediator of God' s kingdom in history. In the messianic era, the nations of the world will proclaim that the God of Israel is king and rules the earth from Mount Zion in Jerusalem.

Thou shalt reign over all whom Thou hast made, Thou alone, O Lord, on Mount Zion, the abode of Thy majesty, in Jerusalem, Thy holy city. (Rosh Ha-Shanah liturgy)

Petitional prayer sustained the biblical focus on history and the broader historical aspirations of the community.

> Our God and God of our fathers, reign over the whole universe in Thy glory; be exalted over all the earth in Thy grandeur; shine forth in Thy splendid majesty over all the inhabitants of Thy world. May every existing being know that Thou hast made it; may every creature realize that Thou hast created it; may every breathing thing proclaim: "The Lord God of Israel is King, and His kingdom rules over all." (Rosh Ha-Shanah liturgy)

God's relational bond to and loving concern for the people Israel were no longer to be judged by Israel's current condition in history. Despite exile and powerlessness, Israel was still God's elect and the recipient of God's special providential concern. Prayer, whether individual or communal, structured a liturgical reality in which God is directly involved with the daily needs of the individual and the community. The following prayer reflects the essence of the central petitional section of the daily Amidah ("Eighteen Benedictions").

> Grant us, Lord our God, wisdom to learn Thy ways; subject our heart to Thy worship; forgive us so that we may be redeemed; keep us from suffering; satisfy us with the products of Thy earth; gather our dispersed people from the four corners of the earth. Judge those who stray from Thy faith; punish the wicked; may the righteous rejoice over the rebuilding of Thy city, the reconstruction of Thy Temple, the flourishing dynasty of Thy servant David and the continuance of the offspring of Thy anointed, the son of Jesse. Answer us

before we call. Blessed art Thou, O Lord, who hearest prayer.

The deep bond between Jews and God, however, was not sustained only through prayer. Daily life was organized around the normative framework of the Torah. Having one's existence all-enveloped by the Halakhah gave to everyday life a deep sense of the ongoing concern and presence of God in the community. The more that different realms of daily life were brought within the scope of Halakhah, the more the community extended and strengthened God's authority in the world.

One of the central pillars of Orthodox Judaism is the belief that the Torah emanated directly from God to Moses. Maimonides formulated it in an uncompromising fashion.

> He who says that the Torah is not of divine origin—even if he says of one verse, or of a single word, that Moses said it of himself—is a denier of the Torah. (*M. T. Laws of Teshuvah* 3:8)

This doctrine must not be understood to mean that pious Jews believe that the account of the Sinai revelation in the Book of Exodus is sufficient to establish the norms for daily living. Revelation does not define the total content of the community's normative life, but only the significance they give to action. All the same, the dogma that every word in the Torah emanates from God taught the religious community that there is no significance to their actions unless they are in response to the divine will. To sense the ongoing commanding will of God in Jewish daily life does not, however, require ongoing revelation. On the contrary, in the classical Orthodox tradition it is human beings, the sages, those who have mastered the tradition through study and loyal practice, who mediate the commanding will of God. The community retains a powerful sense of the authoritative presence of God because it is an interpretive community.

Torah is not only divine law concretized in halakhic rules; it also mediates the uninterrupted speech of God to the community. God's living presence with Israel is expressed not only through normative authority, but also through God's invitation to engage in study of the divine word. "This book of the Torah shall not depart from your mouths, but you shall meditate upon it day and night" (Josh. 1:8). Through the study of Torah, God is not only a commanding will, but equally a live and engaging teacher, calling the community to attentive deliberation and reflection, appealing to the intellect and the imagination to plumb new depths and discover new possibilities of responding to the richness of the divine word.

Meditation on the Torah follows the same pattern described above in relation to the application of Torah law to daily reality. When Jews in the yeshivah study Torah, they do not feel required to open the Book of Leviticus or reflect on the Ten Commandments in order to feel in direct contact with God. They do not need to turn to a page using the language of revelation—"Thus says the Lord"—to feel engaged by God. They may do so equally while studying and reflecting upon a passage of the Talmud in which arguments go back and forth between Hillel and Shammai, Rabbi Johanan and Resh Lakish. In fact, direct study of the biblical text does not at all occupy a central role in the curriculum of advanced yeshivot.

There were rabbinic scholars who ruled that the commandment of studying Torah may be fulfilled without reading the Bible at all—the study of Talmud alone was sufficient to enable the individual to fulfill the commandment to "meditate on God's word day and night."

God is experienced as a living presence when Jews study, when they pray. One senses God's authority in the way

Jews meticulously observe halakhic law. The people of Israel, as an interpretive and learning community, mediates and builds the content of revelation. From the rabbinic tradition onwards, it is the sages who make Torah a living word that brings to the community the living presence of God's kingdom.

This kingdom of Halakhah does not require the support of victorious armies. In the rabbinical academies of learnng, God is not the warrior who manifests power through triumphant victories over Israel's enemies in history. Instead, God is engaged by the joys of studying Torah. Military heroes of the biblical tradition are now portrayed as Torah scholars. Instead of developing ingenious strategies on the battlefield, they are engaged in subtle arguments around the intricacies of halakhic rulings. God's authority and power in history are not reflected in the way Rome, Greece, and Persia respond to God's power. But God rules in full splendor in the house of study. God rules because of the ability of the rabbinic sages to ensure the community's allegiance to the disciplined framework of Halakhah.

Aesthetic experience, too, is channeled into the normative framework of Halakhah, joy into the experience of mitzvah. Human power is exemplified by subordinating one's passions and instincts to the discipline of law. The celebration of the body, the admiration of physical strength, the splendor and glories of nature—these were things that Jews were prepared to leave to the Gentiles. Any crack in this halakhic world of Torah, any doubt that it is intellectually self-sufficient, any flirtation with the wisdom of the Gentiles and their values, would have threatened the delicate but powerful rabbinic vision of Israel's role in history.

> Ben Damah the son of R. Ishmael's sister once asked R. Ishmael: "May one such as I who have studied the whole of the Torah learn Greek wisdom?" He thereupon read to him the following verse: "This book of the Law shall

not depart out of your mouth but you shall meditate therein day and night" (Josh. 1:8). Go then and find a time that is neither day nor night and learn then Greek wisdom. (b. Menahot 99b)

Greek wisdom may only be studied at a time that is neither day nor night. This ironic answer grows out of the full and total claim that Jewish learning must have on its adherents. The culture must be intellectually insulated. Social contact with Gentiles must be kept to a minimum. Laws must be instituted that make social intercourse nearly impossible. The talmudic tractate *Avodah Zarah*, for instance, shows how the rabbis established laws and customs that severely limited all interaction with Gentiles.

In order to generate loyalty to a God who teaches and studies Torah, rather than conquering Israel's enemies, the rabbis built a wall of distrust and cynicism toward anything valued by the political powers of the pagan world. Total commitment to passion for Torah study went hand in hand with repudiating the achievements and political aspirations of the Roman civilization. This is well illustrated by a story about the rabbinic sage Rabbi Simeon Ben Yohai.

R. Judah, R. Jose and R. Simeon were sitting, and Judah, a son of proselytes, was sitting near them. R. Judah commenced by observing: "How fine are the works of this people [the Romans]. They have made streets, they have built bridges, they have erected baths." R. Jose was silent. R. Simeon b. Yohai answered and said: "All of what they made, they made for themselves. They built market-places to set harlots in them; baths, to rejuvenate themselves; bridges, to levy tolls for them." Now, Judah the son of proselytes went and related their talk, which reached the government. They decreed: "Judah, who exalted [us] shall be exalted; Jose, who was silent, shall be exiled to Sepphoris; Simeon, who censured, let him be executed." So they went and hid in a cave. A miracle occurred and a carob-tree and a water well were created for them. They would strip their garments and sit up to their necks in sand. The whole day they studied; when it was time for prayers they robed, covered themselves, prayed, and then put off their garments again, so that they should not wear out. Thus they dwelt twelve years in the cave. Then Elijah came and stood at the entrance to the cave and exclaimed: "Who will inform the son of Yohai that the emperor is dead and his decree annulled?" So they emerged. Seeing a man ploughing and sowing, they exclaimed: "They forsake life eternal and engage in life temporal!" Whatever they cast their eyes upon was immediately burnt up. Thereupon a Heavenly Echo came forth and cried out: "Have ye emerged to destroy My world? Return to your cave!" So they returned and dwelt there twelve months, saying: "The punishment of the wicked in Gehenna is [limited to] twelve months." A Heavenly Echo then came forth and said: "Go forth from your cave!" Thus they issued. . . . R. Phinehas b. Ya'ir his son-in-law heard and went out to meet [R. Simeon]. He took him into the baths and massaged his flesh. Seeing the clefts in his body, he wept and the tears streamed from his eyes. "Woe to me that I see you in such a state!" he cried out. "Happy are you that you see me thus," he retorted, "for if you did not see me in such a state, you would not find me thus [learned]." (b. *Shabbat* 33b)

This story beautifully describes the contrast between the concern with this-worldly activity, with physical beauty and power, and the quest for eternal life gained through exclusive concern with the word of God. Simeon ben Yohai's body is bruised for twelve years. It cannot even be seen, as it is covered by sand. He is pure mind. He joyfully accepts his injured physical condition (i.e., the abandonment of political power) because his suffering (powerlessness) enables him to be single-mindedly devoted to the study of Torah.

Here we see a strong rabbinic tendency to view Halakhah and Torah study as all-embracing and self-sufficient. Many Jews built their traditional culture and communal life around a sacred book; within this text-centered culture, the Jews reflected God's will and majesty through diligent performance of daily mitzvot and devotion to the study of Torah. They may have lived in a world dominated by pagan Rome, but they were taught not to value that world. Everything that is of value could be found within their own tradition. "Ben Bag-Bag said: Study the Torah again and again, for everything is contained in it; constantly examine it, grow old and gray over it, and swerve not from it, for there is nothing more excellent than it" (*Mishnah Avot* 5:25).

R. SOLOVEITCHIK'S INNOVATIVE TRADITIONALISM

R. Soloveitchik could not have attained his position of influence among Orthodox Jews had he not embodied the traditional ideal of total commitment to Torah study. Like Maimonides, R. Soloveitchik captured the Orthodox community's respect because he was an outstanding scholar of Torah. What makes these two masters of Halakhah so perplexing for the traditional Orthodox community is their apparent challenge to the belief in the self-sufficiency of Torah studies. Both R. Soloveitchik and Maimonides brought the wisdom of the world into the inner sanctum of the *beit midrash,* which traditionally had room for Western philosophy "only at a time that is neither day nor night."

R. Soloveitchik and Maimonides threaten the traditional claim of Orthodoxy to intellectual self-sufficiency by demonstrating that a talmudic master need not—indeed, must not—become segregated from world culture. This is why these two thinkers pose such a serious problem for traditional Orthodox commentators. Have they broken down the cultural edifice of intellectual insulation? Have they taken students of Torah beyond their traditional intellectual matrix? Have they introduced alien vocabularies into the self-understanding of halakhic Jews?

The revisionists maintain that R. Soloveitchik was merely a sophisticated apologist for traditional Talmudism. They believe that he merely invoked modern philosophy in order to demonstrate Judaism's intellectual and moral superiority. Certainly, a case can be made for the claim that R. Soloveitchik's halakhic phenomenology, combining classical learning with the Western philosophical tradition, was influenced by the cultural milieu of the early and mid-twentieth century. At that time Orthodoxy was on the defense; modern ideas had seduced many of the brightest talmudic students away from their traditional religious heritage. Conservative and Reform Judaism appeared to offer more appropriate religious structures for American Jewry to grapple with the enormous appeal of the liberal democratic world. Secular culture offered exciting new possibilities that could give direction and meaning to one's life. In that cultural environment it would have been understandable that even an inveterate traditionalist might develop a phenomenology of Halakhah within Western intellectual categories.

The revisionists then go on to claim that this way of defending Judaism is not necessary today. Since then, the cultural climate has changed completely. The triumphant, self-congratulatory ethos of secular culture has been called into question. The widespread sense of personal estrangement and anomie, the loss of rootedness in community, the failure of revolutionary movements, the weakening appeal of secular Zionism in Israel as a viable option for Jewish self-understanding—all these new factors encourage Orthodox Judaism to return to a posture of insulation.

In this new social and political environment, say the revisionists, Judaism must build from within. It must be energized by what has constantly been the source of Judaism's powerful instinct for religious survival throughout history, namely, total repudiation of alien ethical values, delegitimization of anything other than traditionally sanctioned knowledge. Of course, Jews can be part of the world from an economic point of view. They can engage in disciplines and professions that enable them to sustain themselves with dignity. Computer science, mathematics, and the natural sciences can easily be accepted as career options by traditional Orthodox Jews. Western philosophy and literature, however, which go together with the humanistic values of contemporary culture, must be either ignored or repudiated. There is nothing that the religious community needs to learn from this alien intellectual world, and there is no one and no community in the outside world to whom they need feel intellectually accountable. The moral and ethical standards of the West need not concern those who ground their values in their belief in the eternal and absolute truth of the Sinai revelation. Openness to non-Jewish thought and the concern for synthesis and integration within alien bodies of knowledge will in the long run prove destructive to Judaism. The future will be secured only by those educational institutions and rabbinic leaders that insulate Halakhah and the community from Western civilization.

In my view, the revisionists are mistaken. The innovative significance of R. Soloveitchik's thought cannot be measured by his rulings on contemporary halakhic issues. R. Soloveitchik's aggadic reflections, and above all his religious phenomenology, must be given serious weight in any evaluation of his stance on the relationship between the Judaic tradition and modernity. In the coming chapters, I will demonstrate that R. Soloveitchik is the teacher of a new generation of traditional Jews, who believe, in the words of Leo Strauss, that "genuine fidelity to a tradition is not the same as literalist traditionalism, and is in fact, incompatible with it. It consists in preserving not simply the tradition, but the continuity of the tradition."[2]

---

[2]Leo Strauss, *Spinoza's Critique of Religion* (New York: Schocken, 1965), 24.

THE HALAKHIC HERO

WHO IS HALAKHIC MAN?

The title of R. Soloveitchik's first published work in Jewish philosophy, *Ish ha-Halakhah,* or in its English translation, *Halakhic Man,* has generated much confusion. The term "Halakhah" describes a comprehensive way of life forged in the Talmud and subsequent legal codes. The Halakhah comprises a worldview and way of life anchored in Judaism's extensive legal tradition. R. Soloveitchik's title would suggest that he intended to delineate halakhic Judaism's philosophical-religious anthropology. It is thus understandable why Elliot Dorff is so critical of R. Soloveitchik. According to Dorff, R. Soloveitchik's model of halakhic man is not an "empirically accurate" portrayal of either the talmudic tradition or the different types of Jews who live by the Halakhah.

R. Soloveitchik's conceptual imprecision is matched by a similar imprecision in the method with which he treats Biblical and Rabbinic sources. He chooses one midrash that suits his purpose and either ignores sources that make contrary points or he interprets them against their simple meaning.[3]

I will argue that Dorff has misunderstood R. Soloveitchik's project. *Halakhic Man* is neither a historical reconstruction of the rabbinic ethos nor a characterology of the halakhic personality. R. Soloveitchik is not reconstructing the ethos of the talmudic scholars who created the Halakhah. Nor is he describing the characteristic personality engendered by the halakhic way of life. He is not writing an exhaustive phenomenology of "rabbinic man" or "halakhic man" in the broadest sense of those terms. Rather, he is constructing an ideal halakhic type whose approximation is best illustrated by the approach of his father and grandfather to Judaism. Consider the following anecdote, which clearly demonstrates his use of his family's religious tradition for his phenomenology of halakhic man.

> Once my father was standing on the synagogue platform on Rosh Ha-Shanah, ready and prepared to guide the order of the sounding of the shofar. The shofar-sounder, a God-fearing Habad Hasid who was very knowledgeable in the mystical doctrine of the "Alter Rebbe," R. Shneur Zalman of Lyady, began to weep. My father turned to him and said: "Do you weep when you take the lulav? Why then do you weep when you sound the shofar? Are not both commandments of God?" (1983: 60–61)

---

[3]Elliot N. Dorff, "Halakhic Man: A Review Essay," *Modern Judaism* 6, no. 1 (1986): 92–93.

R. Soloveitchik then goes on to explain the difference between the hasidic attitude and his father's.

> [For the Hasid] the sounding of the shofar represents the yearning for the Deus Absconditus whom no thought can grasp, who is separate and removed, awesome and holy. The shofar weeps, wails, and moans over the infinite distance that separates the cosmos from the Ein-Sof, the infinite God. Therefore, it negates the world and raises man to the most absolute transcendent mode of existence. In contrast, the taking of the lulav and the etrog—the fruit of a goodly tree—sustains and affirms the beautiful and resplendent world, which reflects the glory of the God who fills and encompasses all worlds. (1983: 62)

Both R. Soloveitchik's father and the Habad Hasid build their lives around the normative halakhic tradition. Both are "halakhic men," if by that term we designate persons whose religious life is governed by the normative obligations of traditional Judaism. But R. Soloveitchik prefers to use the term "halakhic man" to refer specifically to his father's approach to mitzvot. The Habad Hasid believes that different commandments reflect distinct metaphysical-religious postures. The shofar mirrors a world alienated from God. The lulav, by contrast, reflects a world that embodies the fullness of God. The Hasid thus connects the mitzvah of blowing the shofar with a cosmic yearning for redemption. An organic mythic consciousness infuses his religious life; he believes that mitzvah, God, and the empirical world are interwoven in a cosmic drama of redemption.

Halakhic man, as represented by R. Soloveitchik's father, rejects the hasidic understanding of divine commandments. The significance of mitzvot is for him anchored essentially in the human realm. From halakhic man's formalist perspective, there is no essential difference between the mitzvah of shofar and lulav. Halakhic man refuses to relate either mitzvah symbolically to a cosmic drama mirroring the inner life of divinity; his religious outlook is infused exclusively by the intention to fulfil his duty. As R. Soloveitchik says,

> The Halakhah does not require of us any mystical, esoteric intentions directed towards a *mundus absconditus*, a hidden world, but only the clear, plain thought to fulfill via this particular act such and such a commandment. (1983: 60)

R. Soloveitchik's restricted use of the term "halakhic man" is further exemplified by his grandfather's reaction to the pietistic Lithuanian *musar* movement. The *musar* school of thought emphasized human frailty, the tragedy of the human condition, and the importance of intense introspection.

> The emotion of fear, the sense of lowliness, the melancholy so typical of *homo religiosus,* self-negation, constant self-appraisal, the consciousness of sin, self-lacerating torments, etc., etc., constituted the primary features of the movement's spiritual profile in its early years. It was the practice in Kovno and Slobodka to spend the twilight hour when Sabbath was drawing to a close in an atmosphere suffused with sadness and grief, an atmosphere in which man loses his spiritual shield, his sense of power, confidence, and strength and becomes utterly sensitive and responsive, and there to engage in a monologue about death, the nihility of this world, its emptiness and ugliness. (1983: 74)

Adherents of the *musar* movement recognized that beyond the four cubits of Halakhah there are other realms needed to heal people from sin. They believed that reflection on death and human finitude has a purging influence. They insisted that the Jew cannot build a total religious personality by confining himself or herself entirely within a world of legal texts. R. Isaac Blaser, a leader of the *musar* movement, quoted the following midrash to support his position (1983: 75):

> A man should always incite the good impulse to fight against the evil impulse. . . . If he subdues it, well and good; if not, let him study the Torah. . . . If he subdues it, well and good; if not, let him . . . remind himself of the day of death. (*m. Berakhot* 5a)

R. Soloveitchik recounts how men like his grandfather reacted when an attempt was made to propagate the *musar* movement in their community.

> The halakhic men of Brisk and Volozhin sensed that this whole mood posed a profound contradiction to the Halakhah and would undermine its very foundations. Halakhic man fears nothing. For he swims in the sea of the Talmud, that life-giving sea to all the living. If a person has sinned, then the Halakhah of repentance will come to his aid. One must not waste time on spiritual self-appraisal, on probing introspections, and on the picking away at the "sense" of sin. (1983: 74–75)

R. Soloveitchik's grandfather, Rabbi Hayim, rejected the spirit of fear and melancholy that he found in the *musar* movement. Such a disposition, he believed, detracted from the intrinsically healthy-minded spirit of the halakhic soul.

It should now be clear that R. Soloveitchik's essay *Halakhic Man* is neither a historical analysis of the rabbinic mind in the talmudic era nor a comprehensive discussion of contemporary halakhic spirituality. R. Soloveitchik is a midrashic artist using diverse Judaic strands drawn from the Brisker-Lithuanian tradition of Jewish religiosity to develop a phenomenology of what he sees as an ideal halakhic type. This particular Judaic spiritual type, he believes, was unknown and possibly unintelligible to Western religious thought, which has identified religious life with spiritual asceticism, mystical devotion, and the longing for immortality, characteristics that Soloveitchik lumps together under the definition of *homo religiosus.*

IS R. SOLOVEITCHIK AN APOLOGIST?

At first glance, R. Soloveitchik's preference for the Brisker tradition seems ill-suited for the task of portraying Halakhah in its best light. The religious type exemplified by his grandfather would seem antithetical to the modern sensibility. Western religious thought has greatly focused on the passion for inwardness and the longing for communion with God. Spirituality is generally associated with the religious person's inner quest, the longing for eternity, and the liberation from finitude. The mystic's refined inner life, with its humility, self-effacement, and innocence, has become the standard for evaluating a religion's vitality, significance, and nobility.

By such Western criteria, the Talmud's industrious concern with legal details often appears strange. What happens when someone enters a rabbinic academy and is told that the school will be studying texts that deal with prayer? The opening text in the Mishnah on this subject has the following discussion:

From what time may one recite the Shema in the evening? From the time that the priests enter [their houses] in order to eat their terumah until the end of the first watch. These are the words of R. Eliezer. The sages say: until midnight. R. Gamaliel says: until the dawn comes up. Once it happened that his sons came home [late] from a wedding feast and they said to him: "We have not yet recited the [evening] shema." He said to them: "If the dawn has not yet come up, you are still bound to recite." (*m. Berakhot* 1:1)

What a strange introduction to the life of prayer! One might have expected to find reflections on the unity of God, on the significance of God's kingdom, on the inner parameters of intention and feeling as aspects of the religious quest that should infuse prayer. It is also surprising to see how the rabbinic academy begins to study texts dealing with the festivals and the Sabbath. The Mishnah does not begin with a discussion of the holiness of the festivals of Passover, Shavuot and Sukkot, showing how they embody the significance of God meeting the Judaic community in history. There is no reflection on what it means to celebrate the world as God's creation on the Sabbath or on Rosh Ha-Shanah. Instead of the larger theological questions, we find such strange issues as: What should one do with an egg that was laid on the festival? What may one eat? What may one touch? What activities constitute work? When dealing with the sukkah, the booth that celebrates God's protective love in the desert, the focal questions sound like a builder's manual. How high should a sukkah be? How much covering is required over it? What constitutes a wall? How many walls are needed? One is immediately thrown into the "carpentry" problem! What has happened to the spirit's deep longing for God? How do these technical details express the soul's connection to God?

At first glance, accordingly, the rabbinic academy looks more like a trade school than a religious sanctuary. No wonder that critics of Judaism have portrayed the halakhist as a legalist Pharisee concerned with external forms and oblivious to the inner spiritual world.

R. Soloveitchik's halakhic man seems entirely unappealing to the Western religious thinker. As R. Soloveitchik himself concedes, halakhic man is not especially curious about anything outside the halakhic framework. He lacks an aesthetic sense. The beauty of nature does not capture his attention. He is not concerned with existential issues, such as human mortality and the absurdity of human existence. He shows no interest in metaphysical speculation; the sense of radical wonder, which Aristotle regarded as the beginning of all philosophy (*Metaphysics* 21:A), has no place in his religious life. The existential concerns that normally occupy the religious soul seem totally unrelated to his spiritual lifestyle.

What is there about R. Soloveitchik's seemingly prosaic talmudist that would hold interest for a modern reader? Why would a person versed in Kierkegaard, Barth, and Otto, like R. Soloveitchik himself, be moved by a sober personality that revels in legal-conceptual distinctions?

To be sure, members of the ghettoized yeshivah world, which places a premium on Talmud study, would regard Lithuanian Judaism as a viable religious option. But why should Brisker spirituality appeal to those whose sensibility is shaped by Western philosophical thought? David Singer and Moshe Sokol, in their perceptive article, argue that R. Soloveitchik's religious outlook is not truly modern at all.

> Because "Halakhic Man" is replete with references to the full panoply of Western thinkers and ideas, and because the essay leans heavily on neo-Kantian philosophy, it has been generally assumed that Western thought plays a determinative role in Soloveitchik's

thinking. . . . In fact, however—and this is true of all of Soloveitchik's theological writings—the arrows run in the exact opposite direction; it is Soloveitchik, standing on firm Jewish ground, who uses Western thought to serve his own (Jewish) theological purposes. Thus, as we have seen, "Halakhic Man" is anything but a radical reinterpretation of Judaism in the light of neo-Kantian philosophy. Rather, Soloveitchik latches on to neo-Kantianism as a way of adding to the prestige of talmudism; he dresses up talmudism in neo-Kantian garb so as to make it more appealing to a modern, secularized audience. Soloveitchik's aim in the essay is thoroughly conservative, and he uses neo-Kantian philosophy as a mere packaging device. . . . For Soloveitchik, then, neo-Kantian philosophy specifically and Western thought generally, exist as resource materials to be pressed into the service of Judaism. It is a matter, so to speak, of presenting the old Jewish wine in new westernized bottles.[4]

Singer and Sokol portray R. Soloveitchik's essay as a grand apology for traditional Talmudism. They claim that R. Soloveitchik's allusions to modern philosophy are mere "packaging devices," that is, public relations gimmicks designed to make halakhic Judaism more palatable to the modern reader. Do Singer and Sokol offer a more correct reading of R. Soloveitchik than does Elliot Dorff? Is R. Soloveitchik's essay merely an apology for traditional Judaism? To evaluate these questions, let us examine the central model that R. Soloveitchik uses to illuminate halakhic

---

[4]David Singer and Moshe Sokol, "Joseph Soloveitchik: Lonely Man of Faith," *Modern Judaism* 2, no. 3 (1982): 237–38.

spirituality, namely, the "cognitive man" who delights in mathematics and the natural sciences.

> In order to overcome the mystery in existence, [cognitive man] constructs an ideal, ordered, fixed world, one that is perfectly clear and lucid; he fashions an a priori, ideal creation with which he is greatly pleased. This creation does not cause him any anxiety. It does not attempt to elude him; it cannot conceal itself from him. He knows it full well and delights in the knowledge. Whenever he wishes to orient himself to reality and superimpose his a priori ideal system upon the realm of concrete empirical existence, he comes with his teaching in hand—his a priori teaching. He has no wish to passively cognize reality as it is in itself. Rather, first he creates the ideal a priori image, the ideal structure, and then compares it with the real world. . . . This latter approach is that of mathematics and the mathematical, natural sciences, the crowning achievement of civilization. It is both a priori and ideal—i.e., to know means to construct an ideal, lawful, unified system whose necessity flows from its very nature. (1983: 18–19)

R. Soloveitchik goes on to compare mathematical inventiveness to halakhic consciousness.

> When halakhic man approaches reality, he comes with his Torah, given to him from Sinai, in hand. He orients himself to the world by means of fixed statutes and firm principles. An entire corpus of precepts and laws guides him along the path leading to existence. Halakhic man, well furnished with rules, judgments, and

fundamental principles, draws near the world with an a priori relation. His approach begins with an ideal creation and concludes with a real one. To whom may he be compared? To a mathematician who fashions an ideal world and then uses it for the purpose of establishing a relationship between it and the real world. (1983: 19)

R. Soloveitchik's comparison between Halakhah and mathematics initially appears quite odd. It is hard to understand the similarity between the mathematician's theoretical inquiries and halakhic man's study of talmudic texts.

The Halakhah specifies how Jews should conduct their lives, organize their ritual and practice, and celebrate religiously in their community. It therefore seems inappropriate to view the Halakhah as an a priori construct. Halakhah seems more akin to the model of practical reason than theoretical reason. Aristotle's *Nicomachean Ethics* would seem closer to Halakhah than Euclid's *Elements*. Singer and Sokol claim that R. Soloveitchik introduces this strange analogy in order to present the halakhic legalist in the best light possible. What greater way of dignifying halakhic study than by comparing it, as Soloveitchik does, to mathematics, the "crowning achievement of civilization"? To support their claim that R. Soloveitchik's purpose is essentially apologetic, Singer and Sokol cite his explanation for his use of the mathematical analogy: "I am using this analogy in order to make the whole subject of halakhic man more palatable to scholars of religion who are not familiar with this type" (1983: 146).

How much weight should we attach to the word "palatable"? I will argue that the importance given to the comparison between mathematics and Halakhah in his essay suggests that it is much more than an apology.

To be sure, there are certain apologetic features in R.

Soloveitchik's essay. He clearly seeks to ascribe the highest credit to halakhic Judaism. Some of his praises of it sound hyperbolic. Consider, for example, the following passage:

> No other cognitive discipline has woven crowns for its heroes to the extent that the Halakhah has done. In no other field of knowledge has man been adorned with the crown of absolute royalty as in the realm of Torah. The glorification of man reaches here the peak of splendor. (1983: 81)

As a leader in the Orthodox community, R. Soloveitchik naturally seeks to present halakhic life in its best light. One must also recall that he was writing in a time of crisis for halakhic Judaism. He stood in the midst of a battle against assimilation and indifference, facing a modern world that was deeply seductive to his community. He had to confront an intellectual environment that was drawing the best minds in the Jewish community away from Talmud and Jewish philosophy. Especially in the 1940s and 1950s Orthodox Judaism was under attack from the liberal spirit of openness, personal autonomy, freedom of conscience, and individual self-realization.

Nevertheless, R. Soloveitchik's goal was not merely to adorn the talmudic scholar with the crowns of mathematics and Western philosophy. He was not simply trying to tell the yeshivah student that nothing can compete with the rigor and creativity of talmudic studies. There is something far deeper at stake in R. Soloveitchik's work. His analogy between Halakhah and the cognitive disciplines of Western science is designed to accomplish three goals. First, he seeks to highlight halakhic man's passion for theoretical inquiry. In contrast to the common stereotype, which depicts Judaism as a religion of practice and obedience, R. Soloveitchik shows that halakhic man shares the mathematician's passion for intellectual

34

creativity and rigorous systematic truth. Second, R. Soloveitchik uses this comparison to explain halakhic man's mediated perception of nature. Like the scientist-mathematician, who views natural phenomena through the a priori paradigm of his discipline, halakhic man experiences nature through the normative prism of Halakhah. Third, R. Soloveitchik wishes to suggest that halakhic consciousness can offer an antidote to some dangerous currents of modern thought. The halakhic tradition of sober inquiry can provide a profound answer to the challenge posed to religion by romanticism and existentialism.

THE PASSION FOR THEORETICAL INQUIRY

Judaism has often been compared unfavorably with Greek philosophy. The common stereotype is that Judaism focused on practical morality, while Greek philosophy nurtured the theoretical quest for truth. The Hebrew prophets are known for their moral earnestness, the Greeks for their achievements in mathematics and metaphysics. This understanding of Athens and Jerusalem has recurred throughout the Western philosophical tradition. Even Spinoza, who knew the Jewish tradition, believed that the rabbis lacked philosophical passion. He saw Halakhah purely as a legal-political framework designed to establish a stable social order. Halakhic Judaism, says Spinoza, has no interest in theoretical truth. The human character trait engendered by Torah and Halakhah is not inquisitiveness, but rather, respect for authority. According to Spinoza, Judaism creates a culture of legalist and obedient personalities whose central concern is to maintain political and national stability.

In contrast to this stereotype, R. Soloveitchik demonstrates that theoretical inquiry plays a central role in shaping the talmudic Jew's religious personality. Halakhic society creates an elite class of learned scholars, *talmidei hakhamim*. The esteem due to these scholars is emphasized in familiar talmudic dicta: a learned person born of an illegitimate union is considered more important than a high priest who is ignorant; Jews should value their Torah teachers even more than their parents; standing before a rabbinic scholar is defined as a way of honoring God. One is forbidden to live in a community without schools. Many talmudic texts condemn ignorance and wax enthusiastic about the value of studying Torah. Even God, it is said, spends part of each day studying Torah.

Admittedly, it could be argued that the talmudic emphasis on study is definitely meant for the sake of practice. As the scope of halakhic practice was widened, study became an indispensable guide to behavior. To understand the law and its significance, one had to master a significant corpus of texts. Learning thus emerged as a prerequisite for pious action. *Lo am ha-aretz hasid* ("The ignorant person cannot be fully pious"). One might therefore regard the talmudic emphasis on study as a continuation of the biblical concern with practice.

R. Soloveitchik, however, insists that theoretical inquiry has more than an instrumental value in rabbinic Judaism.

> The foundation of foundations and the pillar of halakhic thought is not the practical ruling but the determination of the theoretical Halakhah. . . . The theoretical Halakhah, not the practical decision, the ideal creation, not the empirical one, represent the longing of halakhic man. (1983: 24)

Halakhic man is not interested only in laws that have practical significance. He also takes a keen interest in talmudic laws that have no bearing on his daily life. Throughout the centuries, rabbinic scholars devoted their attention to laws that had no practical relevance whatsoever. Maimonides, for instance, codified the entire scope of Jewish law, including laws of priestly purity and sacrifices that have had no application for over a thousand years. Subsequent commentators also dealt with laws that could not be implemented in their day.

R. Soloveitchik notes with pride that the rabbinic academies of Brisk and Volozhin studied talmudic tractates that had no relevance for their environment. During the cold winter days in Lithuania, the Brisker halakhists would study agricultural laws pertaining to the Land of Israel. Although no Temple existed, they argued at length over subtle analytic distinctions relating to the laws of Temple sacrifices.

> Halakhic man engages in theoretical discussion and debate concerning the subjects of sacrifice and purity and plumbs the depths of those concepts, laws, and distinctions with the same seriousness that he investigates and searches out the laws of aggunah, plaintiff and defendant, and forbidden foods. The yeshivah of Volozhin introduced the study of the entire Talmud from beginning to end—from Berakhot to Niddah—in place of the previous practice of skipping over those tractates which do not deal with laws that are practiced nowadays. R. Hayim Soloveitchik, aside from his regular lecture at the Yeshivah of Volozhin, would also deliver a parallel lecture on the tractates Zevahim [animal offerings] and Menahot [meal offerings]. . . . When he studied the tractate Berakhot [blessings], he also dealt with agricultural laws, even though those laws, inasmuch as they are dependent upon the land of Israel, are not practiced outside the land. A significant part of his halakhic novella is devoted to laws of sacrifice and purity and defilement. Rabbi Naphtali Zevi Yehudah Berlin acted in a similar fashion, as did many Torah giants before and after them. This stance has been a

fundamental characteristic of halakhists from time im-
memorial. (1983: 24–25)

How can one explain the joy of the Brisker yeshivah student,
who devotes much of his intellectual energy to laws of purity and
sacrifices that have no bearing on his daily existence? These halakhists were not merely preparing themselves for the messianic era,
in which the Temple would be rebuilt. They were not like the mystical hasidic pietists who would sleep with their valises packed because they wanted to be ready for the messianic journey to Israel.

The answer, R. Soloveitchik suggests, lies in halakhic man's
theoretical passion. Halakhic man yearns to understand Torah for
its own sake, *Torah li-shemah*. A yeshivah student studies halakhah
simply because it is an extension of God's word. Swimming in the
intellectual sea of Talmud is a worthy experience in and of itself.
There is something intrinsically significant in creating a coherent
understanding of halakhic legal data. Halakhic man, like the mathematician, has a passion for order, for clarity, for conceptual frameworks that elucidate the entire legal reality of talmudic literature.
His primary concern is to create a coherent conceptual framework
that encompasses the halakhic data, and not necessarily to apply his
intellect to practical affairs.

It is to make sense of this intense intellectual passion that R.
Soloveitchik introduces his analogy between halakhic man and the
creative mathematician. Both mathematician and halakhist rejoice
in their ideally constructed world. Neither is grieved by the fact
that many of these ideal constructions will never be actualized in
empirical reality.

Halakhic man's ideal is to subject reality to the yoke of
Halakhah. However, as long as this desire cannot be
implemented, halakhic man does not despair, nor does

he reflect at all concerning the clash of the real and the ideal, the opposition which exists between the theoretical Halakhah and the actual deed, between law and life. He goes his own way and does not kick against his lot and fate. Such is also the way of the mathematician! When Riemann and Lobachevski discovered the possibility of non-Euclidean space, they did not pay attention to the existential space in which we all live and which we encounter with all our senses, which is Euclidean from beginning to end. They were concerned with an ideal mathematical construction, and in that ideal world they discerned certain features of a geometric space different from ours. (1983: 29)

R. Soloveitchik is well aware that the value of learning for its own sake must compete with another halakhic value: learning for the sake of practice. He knows, on the one hand, that the halakhic tradition recommends study as a means to achieve normative practice. What he also recognizes, on the other hand, is that the halakhic emphasis on study is not exclusively defined by the concerns of practice. The problems of daily life did not define the curriculum for the rabbinic academy. Talmudic scholars were fascinated by materials that had no bearing on their practical affairs.

Since R. Soloveitchik appreciates the energy invested by halakhic scholars in pure theoretical inquiry, he feels justified in offering a bold new interpretation of the talmudic dictum "Great is study, for study leads to action."

Halakhic man is not particularly concerned about the possibility of actualizing the norm in the concrete world. He wishes to mint an ideal, normative coin. Even those laws that are not practiced in the present time are subjected to his normative viewpoint, this despite the fact that he is unable nowadays to fulfill these particular commandments. The maxim of the sages "Great is study, for study leads to action" has a twofold meaning: 1) action may mean determining the Halakhah or ideal norm; 2) action may refer to implementing the ideal norm in the real world. Halakhic man stresses action in its first meaning. (1983: 63–64)

R. Soloveitchik believes that an authentic portrait of Judaism must be drawn not only from talmudic texts, but also from the vital traditions of the rabbinic academy. The yeshivah student's intense interest in laws that have no practical relevance, as well as the community's respect for talmudic scholarship, prove that Jewish learning is not merely a recipe for practice. It is to account for these phenomena that R. Soloveitchik introduces his mathematical analogy. This innovative comparison is not merely apologetic; R. Soloveitchik's goal is to make sense of halakhic man's intense theoretical passion.

ON CREATIVITY AND OBEDIENCE

Throughout his essay, R. Soloveitchik repeatedly insists that the central importance given to halakhic study in the tradition prevents Judaism from becoming a closed legal system demanding passive submission and obedience. Creativity and the pursuit of truth are, for R. Soloveitchik, the cardinal virtues of halakhic Judaism.

Halakhic man received the Torah at Sinai, not as a simple recipient but as a creator of worlds, as a partner with the Almighty in the act of creation. The power of creative interpretation, *hiddush*, is the very foundation of the received tradition. . . .

He does not require any miracles or wonders in order to understand the Torah. He approaches the world of Halakhah with his mind and intellect, just as cognitive man approaches the natural realm. And since he relies upon his intellect, he places his trust in it and does not suppress any of his psychic faculties in order to merge into some supernal existence. His own personal understanding can resolve the most difficult and complex problems. He pays no heed to any murmurings of intuition or other types of mysterious presentiments. (1983: 81, 79)

Intellectual creativity is of the very heart and soul of halakhic man. He longs, above all, for the *hiddush*, the new legal insight. To accomplish his goal, he must rely exclusively on rigorous conceptual analysis. Mystical intuitions are rejected; intimations of grace from above are ignored. Divine intervention in the development of Halakhah violates the integrity and autonomy of halakhic man's intellectual independence.

Halakhic man believes that God has entrusted the understanding of the revelation of Torah to the guidance of human reason. Human deliberation, not prophetic inspiration, mediates the divine word in the rabbinic mind. No longer is man a passive recipient of revelation from above. No longer does God tell man what is required of him. No longer is man asked simply to walk humbly and obediently before God. Rather, he must build a spiritual civilization that grows through his own interpretive skills. God willingly accepts human rule over the direction of Torah. What the earthly court decrees, the Holy One, blessed be He, must accept.

Halakhic man is a mighty ruler in the kingdom of spirit and intellect. Nothing can lead him astray. Everything is subject to him, everything is under his sway and heeds his command. Even the Holy One, blessed be He, has as it were handed over His imprimatur, his official seal in Torah matters, to man. It is as if the creator of the world Himself abides by man's decision and instruction. (1983: 80)

This is a Copernican revolution. A culture that began with theonomy and revelation turns into one in which God obeys and the human judge legislates, in which the Torah scholar is totally free to expand and apply the Torah in accordance with the hermeneutical principles of the talmudic tradition. The literal word of divine revelation becomes, in the hands of the rabbinic sages, an open-textured word, which is shaped in multiple directions.

As the emphasis of Judaism shifts from revelation to the centrality of learning, the entire religious posture changes. The characterology of halakhic man changes from obedience to freedom, from humility to creativity. The revelatory rupture of God into history no longer determines the development of Jewish law. Halakhic knowledge is expanded by human dialogue and the transmission of Torah from one generation to the next. Halakhic man uses his intellectual power to shape his culture. His fundamental allegiance, for R. Soloveitchik, is not to authority, but to truth.

[Halakhic man's] most characteristic feature is strength of mind. He does battle for every jot and tittle of the Halakhah, not only motivated by a deep piety, but also by a passionate love of the truth. He recognizes no authority other than the authority of the intellect (obviously, in accordance with the principles of the tradition). (1983: 79)

To understand R. Soloveitchik's writings in general and *Halakhic Man* in particular, one must appreciate his deep revulsion for intellectual timidity, passivity, and blind obedience—characteristic traits that are normally associated with the religious anthropology of Halakhah.

THE DANGER OF FAUSTIAN MAN

R. Soloveitchik's comparison between mathematics and Halakhah is not designed only to challenge the stereotype of the obedient non-reflective Jew. There is something far more urgent at stake. Through the mathematical analogy, R. Soloveitchik highlights Judaism's sober rule-dominated worldview, its effort to explicate rationally the details of mitzvot, and its concern for expressing religious passion within a fixed, objective, and predictable framework. He thus wishes to show that halakhic Judaism constitutes an antidote to the dangers posed by the modern existentialists, who claimed that subjective passion is the hallmark of religious authenticity.

Philosophers such as Kierkegaard and Nietzsche sought to forge a new model of human excellence by idealizing the heroic individual who stands above society's accepted norms. Authenticity and individuality, they argued, surface only in those who have the courage to live to the extreme. The free spirit must break with the accepted sober patterns of social life and resist the rationalization and collectivization of consciousness that reduce the human being to a tame, crushed, and passive spirit. The new human being will be liberated to the extent that he or she can cast off the inhibiting constraints of scientific rationality. In place of the classical philosophical concern for logical coherence and objective truth,

43

Kierkegaard announces, "Truth is subjectivity." The objective world must be overcome. Our eyes and mind must not be used to discover nature's objective laws. Rather, one must be touched by nature's rich rhythms; the human being must learn to appreciate the passion of subjectivity and inwardness.

R. Soloveitchik shares the respect of the existentialists for the heroic, liberated individual. Yet he also, at the same time, recognizes the dangers posed by the excessive celebration of subjectivity, passion, and spontaneity.

> The sanctification of vitality and intuition, the veneration of instinct, the desire for power, the glorification of emotional-affective life and the flowing, surging stream of subjectivity, the lavishing of extravagant praise on the Faustian type and the Dionysian personality, etc., etc., have brought complete chaos and human depravity to the world. (1983: 141 n. 4)

In *Halakhic Man*, R. Soloveitchik navigates between two poles. On the one hand, he shares the existentialist's appreciation of the hero who rises above bourgeois mediocrity. On the other hand, he distrusts all forms of thought that disparage rational sobriety. At the outset of his essay, R. Soloveitchik announces his profound identification with thinkers such as Kierkegaard, Otto, and Barth, who claim,

> There is a creative power embedded within antithesis; conflict enriches existence; the negation is constructive, and contradiction deepens and expands the ultimate destiny of both man and the world. (1983: 4)

In a long and illuminating footnote on that assertion, R. Soloveitchik explains his reason for citing Kierkegaard, Otto, and Barth. They are cited to

44

give the lie to the position that is prevalent nowadays in religious circles, whether in Protestant groups or in American Reform and Conservative Judaism, that the religious experience is of a very simple nature—that is, devoid of the spiritual tortuousness present in the secular cultural consciousness, of psychic upheavals, and of the pangs and torments that are inextricably connected with the development and refinement of man's spiritual personality. (1983: 139–40 n. 4)

According to R. Soloveitchik, this widespread misperception of the religious personality originates in the mistaken view that religion is "an escape into a realm of simplicity, tranquility and wholeness." It is very revealing to observe that R. Soloveitchik's criticism of Reform and Conservative Judaism focuses neither upon their religious beliefs nor upon their halakhic observance, but upon their religious anthropology. These movements fail to grasp the painful and complex spiritual struggle that characterizes the religious life. Reform and Conservative Judaism are too assimilated to the American ethos, which seeks in religion peace of soul and peace of mind.

Singer and Sokol fail to understand the connection between the opening section of *Halakhic Man,* which enlarges enthusiastically and poetically upon the struggling individual, and the phenomenology of halakhic man found in the rest of the essay.

Why are the theological views expressed in the opening pages of the essay not reflected in the work as a whole; and why, given the fact that they are not reflected there, does Soloveitchik broach them at all in the introduction? The first question is posed with a sense of puzzlement, the second with a feeling of absolute amazement. Could it be that "Halakhic Man" ended up

45

being a very different essay than the one Soloveitchik originally set out to write?[5]

Singer and Sokol are right that halakhic man, as described in the essay, is not caught in conflict and crisis. His world is surrounded by clear normative principles. His perception of the world is firmly anchored. There thus seems to be a radical gap between Kierkegaard's lonely suffering individual and R. Soloveitchik's sober halakhic man. Nevertheless, I believe that R. Soloveitchik's strange introduction provides the key for understanding his project in *Halakhic Man*. By focusing upon Kierkegaard's religious anthropology, R. Soloveitchik is, in effect, telling his readers that he is not writing a philosophy of Jewish law. His essay is not designed, as many claim, to delineate the epistemology of halakhic jurisprudence. Rather, he is defining the characteristics of the halakhic hero.

By celebrating struggle and conflict at the outset of his essay, R. Soloveitchik indicates that he is not articulating a vision of religious life that provides security for the weary spirit. He is not writing for the confused secular person who seeks to find a haven in Judaism. Halakhah is not a refuge for the timid, the frightened, and the weary. It is not an island of safety for those who are afraid to feel the intense contradictions and pains of human existence. Only those capable of loving and feeling intensely, those bold intellectual spirits who do not cower before any authority, whose minds roam freely without feeling the inhibitions of dogmatic authoritarianism—it is for them that R. Soloveitchik writes *Halakhic Man*.

---

[5]Singer and Sokol, "Joseph Soloveitchik," 239–40.

FEATURES OF THE HALAKHIC HERO

Throughout his writings R. Soloveitchik brings his lonely halakhic hero into dialogue with those philosophers who sought to liberate the individual from the chains of mediocrity and conformity. R. Soloveitchik's preoccupation with struggle, suffering, loneliness, and heroic self-overcoming reflects his deep conviction that halakhic Judaism will be a compelling option for modern Jews only if it welcomes the heroic individual and "lonely man of faith" within its communal framework.

Halakhah, to be sure, is not identified with the quest to build a heroic individual. Since Halakhah regulates behavior from the cradle to the grave, it structures through legal rules almost every aspect of human experience. Even the most intimate realms of personal life, such as sexual relationships, dietary habits, and leisure, which one might expect to be left to the individual's determination and initiative, are regulated by explicit halakhic rules.

The halakhic celebration of order and uniform practice seems antithetical to the emphasis upon individualism in modern existentialist thought. The existentialist's concern for the spontaneity and authenticity of the individual seems quite different from the halakhic concern for uniformity of practice in a holy community. Nevertheless, R. Soloveitchik seeks to construct a halakhic personality that shares some of the heroic characteristics heralded by Nietzsche and Kierkegaard, without falling into the dangerous subjectivism of modern philosophy. To understand how R. Soloveitchik develops his model of halakhic heroism, let us return to his analogy between Halakhah and the mathematical sciences.

> God has introduced a parallelism; for just as the qualitative reality to which our senses are exposed lends itself to quantification by cognitive man, who turns qualities into quantities, percepts into equations, so

47

too, the supernal illumination, "which may be perceived by means of the many mighty contradictions which it undergoes as the different levels [of reality] emanate from one another," is placed within and under the dominion of the delimited, "contracted," quantitative act. The "movement" from quality to quantity, from experience to equations, which takes place in the real, empirical world, also finds its expression in the ideal realm of Halakhah. . . . The supernal will is reflected both in the mirror of reality and the mirror of the ideal Halakhah, through the medium of objective, quantitative measurements. (1983: 56–57)

The scientist's model of reality is a measured, ordered, and predictable structure that parallels the empirical world. The scientist's a priori construct filters out the fluctuating, qualitative experience of nature. Just as the scientist-mathematician views nature through the prism of his or her conceptual constructs, so too does halakhic man perceive reality through the mediating framework of halakhic norms. His organs of perception are shaped by a normative framework.

When halakhic man comes across a spring bubbling quietly, he already possesses a fixed, a priori relationship with this real phenomenon, the complex of laws regarding the halakhic construct of a spring. . . . When halakhic man looks to the western horizon and sees the fading rays of the setting sun, or to the eastern horizon and sees the first lights of dawn and the glowing rays of the rising sun, he knows that this sunset or sunrise imposes upon him new obligations and commandments. . . . When halakhic man chances upon mighty

48

mountains, he utilizes the measurements which determine a private domain. . . . When he sees trees, plants
and animals, he classifies them according to their
species and genera. Many laws are dependent upon the
classification of the species. When a fruit is growing,
halakhic man measures the fruit with the standards of
growth and ripening that he possesses. (1983: 20–21)

Through his strange and austere descriptions of halakhic
man's encounter with nature, R. Soloveitchik is constructing a
human type whose total perception of reality is controlled by the
normative halakhic framework. Every contact with nature that
might inspire aesthetic enthusiasm is channeled through the functional halakhic question: What mitzvot, what new obligations does
this phenomenon awaken? How does ritual purification become
possible through this spring? How are these mountains related to
the categories of private and public domains, which are important
for the laws of the Sabbath? What blessings must I recite over these
fruits? When are these fruits subject to the law of tithes? What stage
of vegetative growth must they reach in order for me to fulfill my
normative obligations?

For R. Soloveitchik, the mitzvot do not merely determine
how one acts; they also orient one's overall understanding of God,
humankind, and the world. The norm is not extraneous to halakhic
man's being; it is the prism through which he perceives reality. Divine commandments are the central framework of halakhic man's
reality. The normative discipline imposed by God is the center of
his world. His sense of duty fills his entire being; halakhic man's
basic concern is to infuse all of reality with the Halakhah. Halakhah
defines not only what halakhic man will see, but also the emotions
with which he responds to prosperity and tragedy. As an example,
R. Soloveitchik recalls the behavior of the Gaon of Vilna.

It is related concerning the Gaon of Vilna how greatly he would rejoice on Simhat Torah during the *hakafot*. He would dance, clap, sing, and celebrate the occasion in a state of great rapture and enthusiasm. However, immediately afterward, upon the conclusion of the *hakafot*, he would revert back to his normal tranquil state. When the Gaon's brother died and the Gaon learned of it on the Sabbath [when mourning is forbidden], he did not display any emotion or signs of grief. After the Sabbath, when he concluded the *havdalah*, he burst into tears. (1983: 77)

The Gaon of Vilna is capable of intense feelings, as is revealed the moment the Sabbath is over. But on the Sabbath, when public mourning is forbidden, his feelings are totally subsumed by the Halakhah. He can dance jubilantly when there is a mitzvah to rejoice. But as soon as the obligation is over, one cannot discern even an afterglow of joy. For the Gaon of Vilna, joyful and tragic emotions surface only within the structured framework of Halakhah.

The halakhic control of emotions is further illustrated in a dramatic anecdote about R. Elijah Pruzna, whom R. Soloveitchik celebrates as a paradigm of halakhic heroism.

The beloved daughter of Elijah Pruzna [Feinstein] took sick about a month before she was to be married and after a few days was rapidly sinking. R. Elijah's son entered into the room where R. Elijah, wrapped in *tallit* and *tefillin,* was praying with the congregation, to tell him that his daughter was in her death throes. R. Elijah went into his daughter's room and asked the doctor how much longer it would be until the end. When he received the doctor's reply, R. Elijah returned to his room, removed his Rashi's *tefillin,* and quickly put on the *tefillin* prescribed by Rabenu Tam, for immediately upon his daughter's death, he would be an *onen,* a mourner whose dead relative has not yet been buried, and as such would be subject to the law that an *onen* is exempt from all the commandments. After he removed his second pair of *tefillin,* wrapped them up, and put them away, he entered his dying daughter's room, in order to be present at the moment his most beloved daughter of all would return her soul back to its Maker. (1983: 77–78)

There is something abnormal—one might even say inhuman—about R. Elijah's behavior. One would normally expect a father to want to be with his daughter in her final moments. When a child is dying, one would not expect a father to worry about such questions as, What mitzvot will I be able to perform when my status changes to a mourner? Will I be able to put on my second pair of *tefillin?* One would expect a father to be engrossed entirely by his immediate tragedy and by the basic human need to comfort his daughter, if only by a loving glance and expression of love. Nevertheless, R. Soloveitchik regards R. Elijah as a paradigm of halakhic man. His reaction to his daughter's death exemplifies "great strength and presence of mind, the acceptance of the divine decree with love, the consciousness of the law and the judgment, the might and power of the Halakhah, and faith strong like flint" (1983: 78).

Such stories evoke an eerie, even repugnant, feeling in me for R. Elijah. Where is the human "I," the individual in R. Soloveitchik's halakhic hero? Has he become a machinelike personality? Has he lost all the natural feelings of a parent for a child? Either one reacts with disgust at halakhic man's regimented and rule-bound personality or one feels to be in the presence of a unique personality who refuses to be carried along by the currents of human feelings. The response to halakhic man is either a profound "No!" or a feeling that one is standing before someone quite extraordinary and special. It is impossible to remain neutral. This sense of either/or is precisely what R. Soloveitchik intends to create. His halakhic man does not share the sensibilities of what we normally expect of the religious person. These bizarre and strange stories reflect R. Soloveitchik's deep concern not to identify halakhic man with the bourgeois religious personality who joins the church or synagogue to find some tranquility.

A FLAWLESS HERO?

Reading R. Soloveitchik's essay, one wonders, Does halakhic man's orderly world ever break down? What about halakhic man's sense of his own mortality? Do the morbid, painful, and tragic dimensions of the human condition ever invade his awareness? Do intimations of his finitude unsettle his ordered, normative world? Can they propel him into a state of loneliness and alienation from the community? The existentialists, with their celebration of subjectivity, believed that the encounter with tragedy and the recognition of mortality liberates people from the cage of social conformity. Death, they claimed, awakens a person to his or her singleness. In contrast to the existentialist hero, however, halakhic man is left untouched by experiences of nothingness, chaos, death, and the absurd.

> Such concepts as nothingness and naught, chaos and the void, darkness and the abyss are wholly foreign to him [halakhic man]. . . . Halakhic man is a man of the law and the principle, a man of the statute and the judgment, and, therefore, he always possesses in his being, even if at times it should be afflicted with a deep

melancholy, a fixed, firm, Archimedean point that is outside and above the turbulence of his soul, beyond the maelstrom of the affective life, a true source of peace and tranquillity. Halakhic man vanquishes even the fear of death, which, as was explained above, is rooted in his world perspective, by means of the law and the Halakhah, and he transforms the phenomenon, which so terrifies him, into an object of man's observation and cognition. For when death becomes an object of man's cognition, the fright accompanying death dissipates. Death is frightening, death is menacing, death is dreadful only so long as it appears as a subject confronting man. However, when man succeeds in transforming death-subject into death-object, the horror is gone. My father related to me that when the fear of death would seize hold of R. Hayyim, he would throw himself, with his entire heart and mind, into the study of the laws of tents and corpse defilement. And these laws, which revolve about such difficult and complex problems as defilement of a grave, defilement of a tent, blocked-up defilement, interposition before defilement, a vessel with a tight-fitting cover upon it in a tent in which a corpse lies, etc., etc., would calm the turbulence of his soul and would imbue it with a spirit of joy and gladness. When halakhic man fears death, his sole weapon wherewith to fight this terrible dread is the eternal law of the Halakhah. The act of objectification triumphs over the subjective terror of death. (1983: 72–73)

The functional utilitarian marketing of religion breaks down before the awesome figure of halakhic man, whose entire personality is pervaded by a normative framework. Judaism is not a tangential feature of his consciousness. The normative world of Judaism invades every corner of his existence. The passion to "halakhasize" life is total. R. Soloveitchik makes halakhic man into a Promethean figure who superimposes his normative framework upon all of reality. There is no entry of chaos. There are no surprises. There is no invasion of nonrational forces into his consciousness. The halakhic hero is the law; he has no affective and behavioral life separate from the law. Herein lies the key to understanding R. Soloveitchik's puzzling claim that halakhic man experiences no conflict with the law.

> Halakhic man does not struggle with his evil impulses, nor does he clash with the temptor who seeks to deprive him of his senses. . . . Unlike the Christian saints whose lives consisted of a long series of battles with the dazzling allure of life, with carnal, this-worldly pleasures, the great Jewish scholars know nothing about man's conflict with the evil urge. The church fathers devoted themselves to religious life in a state of compulsion and duress, the Jewish sages in a state of joy and freedom. . . . We do not have here a directive that imposes upon man obligations against which he rebels, but delightful commandments which his soul passionately desires. (1983: 65)

Elliot Dorff takes R. Soloveitchik to task on this point.

> Soloveitchik's staunchly theoretical stance misleads him not only in regard to the nature of Jewish law; it also leads him to embrace an odd, and frankly un-Jewish view of mankind. He says that Halakhic man has no desire to act against the law since the Halakhah is written into his being. . . . How helpful is it to describe

"Halakhic Man" in a way which even the tradition proclaimed was beyond the capacity of normal, halakhically observant people? . . . Moreover, according to
one famous Rabbinic source, it is not ideal for Halakhic man to lack desire to transgress the law; he
should rather have strong urges to transgress it but observe it nevertheless as a mark of his fealty to God.[6]

At first glance, Dorff's point seems well taken. R. Soloveitchik's description of halakhic man seems identical to what Nachmanides says Jews can become only in the utopia of the messianic
age, when they will experience no temptation to transgress the law.

But in the days of the Messiah, the choice of their
[genuine] good will be natural; the heart will not desire the improper and it will have no craving whatever
for it. . . . Man will return at that time to what he was
before the sin of Adam, when by his nature he did what
should properly be done, and there were no conflicting desires in his will. (*Commentary to Deut.* 30:6)

On careful analysis, however, it becomes evident that R.
Soloveitchik's halakhic man has little in common with Nachmanides' messianic-utopian man, or for that matter, with
Jeremiah's and Ezekiel's visions of a new spirit and a new heart. R.
Soloveitchik is not describing a messianic personality; he is describing halakhic man's life in an unredeemed world. How, then, can we
make sense of his claim that halakhic man, unlike the Christian
saint, does not obey the law from a spirit of compulsion?

First, it must be emphasized again that R. Soloveitchik is

---

[6]Dorff, "Review Essay," 95.

describing the ideal halakhic hero, not the normal halakhic Jew. Second, halakhic man, through his talmudic mastery, exploits the enormous range of interpretive freedom found within the tradition. His total intellectual energy is devoted to expounding the law. Third, he perceives reality through his a priori halakhic constructs. In living in accordance with the rulings of this law, therefore, he believes that he is giving expression to his own intellectual autonomy. He lives by a law that has been shaped and formed by his own intellect. The law, therefore, does not appear extraneous to his identity. There is no conflict with the law, because he has no feelings and identity separate from the law.

The real world does not impose upon him anything new, nor does it compel him to perform any new action of which he had not been aware beforehand in his ideal world. And this ideal world is his very own, his possession. He is free to create in it, to arrive at new insights, to improve and perfect. Spiritual freedom and intellectual independence reign there in unlimited fashion.

THE KANTIAN PARALLEL

Israeli philosopher Avishai Margalit raised the question whether halakhic man's sense of freedom and autonomy is anything more than a sophisticated exercise in self-deception. Is it not possible to apply R. Soloveitchik's argument to exalt any oppressed way of life? Is halakhic man not like the slave described in Exodus who refuses to accept freedom when his period of servitude has ended because he identifies totally with his master's way of life?

> If his master gave him a wife, and she has borne him children, the wife and her children shall belong to the master, and he shall leave alone. But if the slave declares, "I love my master, and my wife and children;

I do not wish to go free," his master shall take him before God. He shall be brought to the door or the door-
post, and his master shall pierce his ear with an awl;
and he shall then remain his slave for life. (Exod.
21:4–6)

The Bible punishes the Hebrew slave who prefers the security of his
master's home to the uncertainty of freedom. It does not allow the
slave's love for his master's home or even for his own family to blur
the boundaries between slavery and freedom.

R. Soloveitchik echoes Kantian vocabulary when he describes halakhic man as an autonomous actor in the moral sphere.

The goal of self-creation is individuality, autonomy,
uniqueness, and freedom. However, as was explained
earlier, the complete freedom of the man of God is
embodied in his perception of the norm as an existential law of his own individual and spiritually independent being; he discovers his freedom in the halakhic
principle, which is deeply rooted in his pure soul. For
this norm, this principle is unaccompanied by any
sense of compulsion, and a person does not feel "as
though he were compelled by some mysterious, hidden
power." Rather he rejoices in its fulfillment and realization. (1983: 135–36)

The Kantian ethical system indeed defines dignity in terms of
autonomy, spontaneity, and creativity. R. Soloveitchik, however,
cannot operate in a revelatory system with the Kantian notion of
moral autonomy. Through revelation, the source of authority is
God, embodying what Kant would call a heteronomous principle of
morality. R. Soloveitchik must therefore reject the idea that human
beings are capable of developing their own system of norms.

This concept of freedom should not be confused with the principle of ethical autonomy propounded by Kant and his followers. The freedom of the pure will in Kant's teaching refers essentially to the creation of the ethical norm. The freedom of halakhic man refers not to the creation of the law itself, for it was given to him by the Almighty, but to the realization of the norm in the concrete world. The freedom which is rooted in the creation of the norm has brought chaos and disorder to the world. The freedom of realizing the norm brings holiness to the world. (1983: 153 n. 80)

R. Soloveitchik's fundamental thesis is that Kant's distinction between heteronomy and autonomy breaks down in a revelatory system that makes the study of Torah the central framework of its religious life. The total freedom of the man of God is embodied in his perception of the norm, not in its creation. "He desires the Torah of God, and in his Torah does he meditate day and night" (Ps. 1:2) What begins as the "Torah of God" becomes for halakhic man "his Torah," albeit not in the Kantian sense. Halakhic man is not the self-legislating creator of norms. However, Torah study generates the sense that law is a direct expression of halakhic man's individuality and independence.

It is astonishing that an objective authoritarian system, which demands total allegiance and complete submission to the divine will, can nevertheless be felt by its practitioners to celebrate and glorify human independence, spontaneity, freedom, and creativity. For R. Soloveitchik, this is the authentic phenomenology of Halakhah. The outsider sees Halakhah as a system of constraints and inhibitions that crush spontaneity and personal freedom. Inside the system, however, halakhic man does not feel inhibited by extraneous norms. He senses not coercion but subjective freedom, for the entire framework of Halakhah is really his own creation.

R. Soloveitchik has appropriated Kant's notion of individual dignity for halakhic man, even though halakhic man's morality is heteronomous in the original Kantian sense. The Kantian critique of heteronomy is then directed by R. Soloveitchik at *homo religiosus,* the Western and especially Christian ideal religious type, whose otherworldly spiritual orientation develops passivity, submissiveness, and the need for grace in order to feel accepted by God. It is halakhic man, as contrasted to *homo religiosus,* who has an autonomous personality. Creativity flows from his faith in his own intellectual powers.

What is important for R. Soloveitchik is not the source of the authority of the norm but how one appropriates it. One can appropriate Kant's view of human dignity, while at the same time embracing the Orthodox belief that every single word in the Torah was directly revealed by God (see the formulation of Maimonides in the previous chapter). Uniqueness, creativity, and self-discovery are experientially present in the halakhic way of life. Halakhic man may begin his spiritual life as a heteronomous personality, but he ends up becoming totally autonomous.

This is also how R. Soloveitchik's essay "Redemption, Prayer, Talmud Torah" uses the midrash that describes how every infant studies all of the Torah before birth, but loses that precious memory in the process of being born. The student of Torah is like the amnesia victim who tries to reconstruct from fragments the beautiful world he or she once experienced. By learning Torah, man returns to his own self. The centrality of Torah study in the talmudic tradition transmutes the heteronomous Halakhah into an autonomous spiritual worldview. For Avishai Margalit, halakhic man's sense of autonomy is bad faith and a return to slavery. For R. Soloveitchik, it is joy, freedom, and independence.

THE HALAKHIC HERO

The themes of heroism, loneliness, and individual self-realization accompanied R. Soloveitchik throughout the years of his theological reflections. In his essay "The Community," written many years after *Halakhic Man*, Soloveitchik explicitly proclaimed heroism as the central category of Judaism.

> The originality and creativity in man are rooted in his loneliness-experience, not in his social awareness. . . . Lonely man is profound. He creates. He is original. Lonely man is free; social man is bound by many rules and ordinances. God willed man to be free. Man is required from time to time, to defy the world, to replace the old and obsolete with the new and relative. Only lonely man is capable of casting off the harness of bondage to society. . . . Heroism is the central category in practical Judaism. (1978a: 13)

Nietzsche's heroic type frees himself from mediocrity by gaining the ability to express his passionate feelings without restraints. R. Soloveitchik's hero does so by channeling his passionate feelings through the discipline of Halakhah. In R. Soloveitchik's essay "Catharsis," the halakhic hero is likewise portrayed in antithesis to the celebration of spontaneity. According to halakhic law, a mourner must stop his public observance of mourning if a festival occurs during his intense period of grief. What takes place in the heart of the mourner as he meets this halakhic requirement?

> The mourner, who has buried a beloved wife or mother, returns home from the graveyard where he has left part of himself, where he has witnessed the mockery of human existence. He is in a mood to question

the validity of our entire axiological universe. The house is empty, dreary, every piece of furniture reminds the mourner of the beloved person he has buried. Every corner is full of memories. Yet the Halakhah addresses itself to the lonely mourner, whispering to him: "Rise from your mourning; cast the ashes from your head; change your clothes; light the festive candles; recite over a cup of wine the Kiddush extolling the Lord for giving us festivals of gladness and sacred seasons of joy; pronounce the blessing 'Blessed art Thou . . . who has kept us in life and has preserved us to reach this season'; join the jubilating community and celebrate the holiday as if nothing had transpired, as if the beloved person over whose death you grieve were with you." . . . Let us repeat the question: Is such a metamorphosis of the state of mind of an individual possible? Can one make the leap from utter bleak desolation and hopelessness into joyous trust? Can one replace the experience of monstrosity with the feeling of the highest meaningfulness? I have no right to judge. However, I know of people who have attempted to perform this greatest of all miracles. This leap is certainly heroic. It is less spectacular than the death of an Achilles; yet it is more heroic, more redeeming, because it is performed in humility and in the hush of a dark night of loneliness. (1978c: 49–50)

Kierkegaard's hero, the single one, rebels against institutional religiosity. R. Soloveitchik, in contrast to many existentialists, charts a new path. He does not set up an opposition between the heroic individual and the community; nor does he contrast spontaneity with the intellectual quest for objectivity; nor does he regard heroism as incompatible with an ordered framework of normative existence.

Is R. Soloveitchik trying to square the circle? Can heroic self-realization be reconciled with a halakhic way of life that disciplines one's behavior from the cradle to the grave? Can the democratic normative emphasis of halakhic Judaism walk hand in hand with *Halakhic Man*'s elitist portrayal of the scholarly hero? This is the difficult issue with which R. Soloveitchik's writing constantly grappled. This, and no mere apologetics, explains his ongoing discussion with Kierkegaard, Nietzsche, Otto, and Barth. R. Soloveitchik's religious anthropology consequently poses a far-reaching educational challenge not just for Orthodox Judaism but for any religious system that seeks to integrate the modern understanding of human dignity and individuality with commitment to community and tradition.

3

THE RELIGIOUS PASSION OF

HALAKHIC MAN

THE UNIQUENESS OF HALAKHIC MAN

In the opening passages of *Halakhic Man*, R. Soloveitchik asserts, "The image that halakhic man presents is singular, even strange. He is of a type that is unfamiliar to students of religion" (1983: 3). At first, it might appear that R. Soloveitchik is merely saying that students of religion influenced by Christian patterns of thought are not familiar with the type of religious experience found in traditional Judaism, or at any rate in its talmudic Lithuanian form. In reading the essay carefully, however, we discover that R. Soloveitchik has something far more radical in mind.

> Halakhic man's approach to reality is, at the outset, devoid of any element of transcendence. Indeed, his entire attitude to the world stands out by virtue of its originality and uniqueness. All of the frames of reference constructed by the philosophers and psychologists of

religion for explaining the varieties of religious experience cannot accommodate halakhic man as far as his reaction to empirical reality is concerned. (1983: 17)

Halakhic man's singularity and strangeness are not to be attributed solely to unfamiliarity. R. Soloveitchik makes the stronger claim that the psychological and philosophical categories prevailing in academic religious studies are not adequate for making sense of halakhic man. Let us examine, therefore, R. Soloveitchik's claim that halakhic man's relationship to God or transcendence is unique.

In the previous chapter, it was shown that halakhic man's spiritual life is nurtured by two central features of the Judaic tradition. One is the mitzvot, the practical commandments through which God is mediated and revealed to the community. The other is Torah study. The Judaic community's way of life is defined by the entire exegetical tradition, not merely by the Bible's revelatory framework. As portrayed by R. Soloveitchik, halakhic man lives in intense discussion and dialogue with two thousand years of commentary by Torah scholars who participated in the development and clarification of Halakhah.

R. Soloveitchik discerns a profound dialectic between revelation and intellectual creativity. Although halakhic man believes that every word of Torah is divine, this very word itself becomes his possession and plaything. There is both receptivity and creativity in halakhic Judaism. All authority is grounded in divine revelation, yet even God submits to the earthly academy's ruling. The law is shaped, interpreted, and expanded by halakhic man, not by prophets claiming the authority of revelation. Halakhic man repudiates any suggestion that revelatory grace is necessary for interpreting Torah. This learning tradition enables halakhic man to feel intellectually adequate and self-confident. Nothing beyond ordinary human resources is needed to provide normative guidance for the covenantal community of Israel.

Halakhic man's sense of autonomy is not simply a psychological experience arising from his identification with and internalization of God's revealed law. The Torah scholar's sense of autonomy is above all based upon the fact that it is human interpreters who define the halakhic norm's applicability and content. R. Soloveitchik illustrates the point with familiar passages from the Midrash. When the ministering angels ask God on what days Rosh Ha-Shanah and Yom Kippur will fall, when God will judge Israel, God tells them to heed the decision of Israel's earthly court. As R. Judah inferred from "These are the festivals of the Lord, which you shall proclaim" (Lev. 23:4), "God said: 'Before Israel became My people, the festivals were the festivals of the Lord.' But henceforth the festivals are those 'which you shall proclaim'" (*Deut. Rab.* 2:24). Another passage compares the relationship between God and Israel with that between a king, who had treasure houses filled with every precious thing, and his only son. "When the son grew up and came of age, his father told him: 'As long as you were a minor, I would watch over everything. Now that you have come of age, I am handing over everything to you'" (*Exod. Rab.* 15:30). R. Soloveitchik comments,

> The Holy One, Blessed be He, has, as it were, stripped Himself of His ornaments—i.e., His dominion—and has handed it over to Israel, to the earthly court. The earthly court decrees, and the Holy One, blessed be He, complies. If the earthly court rules in matters of law and judgment, the Halakhah is always in accordance with its decision, even if the heavenly court should disagree. Halakhic man reigns over all and is esteemed by all. (1983: 81)

HOMO RELIGIOSUS:
THE ANTITHESIS OF HALAKHIC MAN

R. Soloveitchik highlights the unique earthbound features of halakhic man by contrasting him with another ideal type, *homo religiosus*, who is indeed familiar to Western students of religion. Of the latter, he says,

> He seeks to discover the source of plenitude in being and of the fullness of the cosmos in supernal ontic realms that are pristine and pure. This transcendent approach to reality constitutes a primary feature of the profile of the man of God. *Homo religiosus* is dissatisfied, unhappy with this world. He searches for an existence that is above empirical reality. This world is a pale image of another world. . . .
>
> The ethical and religious ideal of *homo religiosus* is the extrication of his existence from the bonds of this world, from the iron chains of empirical reality, its laws and judgments, and its elevation up to the level of being of a higher man in a world that is wholly good and wholly eternal. (1983: 13, 15)

The quest of the mathematical scientist, who, for R. Soloveitchik, typifies "cognitive man," to understand nature does not require him to posit a mysterious transcendental source of being. By contrast, the spiritual quest of *homo religiosus* leads him inevitably beyond the empirically given. *Homo religiosus* regards the empirical world as a transparent representation of something more ultimate, mysterious, and awesome.

Cognitive man feels fully at home in a universe governed by his empirical laws. *Homo religiosus* feels displaced; he is not in his true home as long as he is trapped in the given framework of the natural world. The one is at home in the temporal; the other in the eternal. The one remains fully anchored in finitude; the other longs to be absorbed by the infinite.

> *Homo religiosus*, dissatisfied, disappointed, and unhappy, craves to rise up from the vale of tears, from concrete reality, and aspires to climb to the mountain of the Lord. He attempts to extricate himself from the narrow straits of empirical existence and emerge into the wide spaces of a pure and pristine transcendental existence. . . .
>
> *Homo religiosus*, who thirsts for the living God, demolishes the bounds of this-worldliness, transforms himself into pure spirit, breaks through all barriers, and ascends on high. For him the approach to God consists in a leap from the empirical and concrete into the transcendent and the mysterious. (1983: 40, 45)

For *homo religiosus*, the concrete material world is an affront to divinity; the temporal fleeting moment is the total antithesis to the longing for eternal life. The longing for holiness, redemption, and purity is consummated only to the extent that the finite, temporal, human world is totally transcended and absorbed by God's mysterious, infinite, redeeming power. Death is the portal conveying man from a limited mortal existence to an eternally blessed life of salvation.

Homo religiosus yearns to be released from the chains of matter; he strives to become pure spirit; he longs for a world free from all human contradictions and distractions. *Homo religiosus* feels like a stranger in his body and in human history. He believes that the *Shekhinah*, the Divine Presence, cries out in exile as it is trapped in the finite material world. The human task is to liberate God and human individuals from the sinful blemish of temporality, finitude, and concreteness.

> The mystic sees the existence of the world as a type of "affront," heaven forbid, to God's glory; the cosmos, as it were, impinges upon the infinity of the Creator. . . .
>
> The desire of mystical doctrine is to free both man and the *Shekhinah*, the Divine Presence, from the world and from the visible reality which is imprinted with the stamp of the supernal. (1983: 49, 51)

Religion and God provide a vital consolation for those who experience the world in this way. The longing for eternal salvation provides a powerful alternative to life's struggles and imperfections. God provides an escape from the limitations of history and the body. *Homo religiosus* believes that secular atheism locates humankind's true home in a fleeting, corrupt realm. By contrast, he believes, theism describes an eternal, perfect abode, which represents the true destiny of the human spirit. For *homo religiosus,* ethics and politics merely provide an orientation to this world. Religion offers worship symbols, rituals, and experiences through which one becomes aware that this world is simply a vestibule to a realm far more ultimate and significant.

R. Soloveitchik is well aware that halakhic man's attitude to the world seems closer to secular man than to *homo religiosus.* Halakhic man is not overwhelmed and tortured by the weight of human sinfulness and pride. He is not a spiritual beggar seeking divine forgiveness for his human limitations. The self-sufficient confidence revealed in the academy of Torah learning inspires him with the belief that whenever he knocks at the gates of heaven, he will be answered. The study of Torah generates the conviction that God is always present for those who seek him. He therefore does not feel the need for intermediaries or holy persons to mediate his connection with divinity. "Every individual is assured by the Halakhah that whenever he will knock on the gates of heaven, they will be opened before him" (1983: 43).

This self-confidence is not born from religious innocence and naiveté. R. Soloveitchik repeats often in his essay that halakhic man is fully awake to the contradictions and struggles present in the religious experience. For instance, R. Soloveitchik's halakhic man is aware of the deep antithesis and ambivalence found in the Psalms. In Psalm 2 the human being is hailed as a uniquely significant being, "Thou hast made him little lower than the angels" (Ps. 2:8), but at the same time is reminded, "What is man that Thou are mindful of him?" (Ps. 2:7). Human beings are dust and clay who vanish quickly from this earth; they are like a dry leaf, which the wind blows about in all directions. Yet humankind is also the crowning achievement of creation. Both *homo religiosus* and halakhic man are aware of this fundamental tension in the religious life. For *homo religiosus*, however, a painful alternation between self-affirmation and self-negation is humankind's permanent lot.

> From a religious perspective, man, in his relationship to the world, oscillates between the two poles of self-negation and absolute pride, between the consciousness of his nothingness and the consciousness of the infinity deep within him. *Homo religiosus* can never be free of this oscillation. (1983: 68)

This vacillation between self-affirmation and total self-negation is the lot of *homo religiosus*. Halakhic man, by contrast, has a way of liberating himself from this painful tension within the human condition. R. Soloveitchik insists that, by placing mitzvah at the center of religious consciousness, Judaism offers the possibility of overcoming the paradox that perplexes *homo religiosus*. The commandments make sense only if we see them as reflecting God's confidence in the capacities of human beings to take responsibility for building a holy kingdom on earth.

The extent to which mitzvah mediates halakhic man's feeling of acceptance and self-worth is dramatically portrayed in R. Soloveitchik's description of the closing prayers of Yom Kippur.

> Halakhic Man . . . in the climactic *Ne'ilah* prayer, confesses his sins before his Creator. He begins: "What are we? What is our life? What is our goodness? What is our virtue? . . . " And in truth, what is man when set against the vast universe and the heavenly realms? . . . And a deep, hidden anxiety seizes hold of him; a great dread springs upon him and nullifies his being and selfhood. He is overcome by despair; filled with loathing and self-contempt. However, at that very moment one thought flashes through his mind. If "man hath no pre-eminence above a beast; for all is vanity," then what is the nature of the Day of Atonement? . . . Why should we be confronted at all with the concept of sin and iniquity on the one side and the obligation to repent on the other? . . . Indeed, the Halakhah set man at the very center of its world, and the Day of Atonement testifies to this. . . . God commanded man, and the very command itself carries with it the endorsement of man's existence. . . . The Day of Atonement which was given unto us in love, the promise of pardon and forgiveness, the obligation to repent, the existence of the statutes which God has willed are the clearest and strongest testimony to man's importance, his central place in the world. (1983: 69–71)

70

THE INTEGRATIVE PERSONALITY

The realm of mitzvot does not create a split between soul and body. There is an integrative experience in which humankind is told that the total person can be brought into the religious life. The laws governing food and sex are not seen by R. Soloveitchik as a repudiation of the body or a way of minimizing the joys of physical existence. They are intended to sanctify and celebrate the biological functioning of the body, to encourage human beings not to become alienated from their own natural existence, but to feel that all that is human can be brought into the presence of God.

> If you desire an exoteric, democratic religiosity, get thee unto the empirical, earthly life, the life of the body with all its two hundred forty-eight organs and three hundred sixty-five sinews. Do not turn your attention to an exalted spiritual life rooted in abstract worlds. . . .
>
> Holiness consists of a life ordered and fixed in accordance with Halakhah and finds its fulfillment in the observance of the laws regulating human biological existence, such as the laws concerning forbidden sexual relations, forbidden foods and similar precepts. (1983: 44, 46–47)

Maimonides understood the motifs of purity and holiness associated with these commandments in the following way:

> To the totality of the purposes of the perfect Law there belong the abandonment, depreciation, and restraint of desires in so far as possible, so that these should be satisfied only in so far as this is necessary. . . . Consequently He states clearly that sanctity consists in

71

renouncing sexual intercourse, just as He also states explicitly that the giving up of the drinking of wine constitutes sanctity. (*Guide for the Perplexed* 3:35)

R. Soloveitchik, by contrast, does not see the suppression of human physical and sensuous instincts as the rationale for these commandments. The vitality of human sensuous passions and bodily drives need not be crushed in order to achieve holiness and purity. R. Soloveitchik's halakhic affirmation of human biological-material existence is very far from the Aristotelian conception, shared by Maimonides, in which the true essence of a human being lies in the intellect. Halakhah also differs from the Platonic conception that the task of philosophy is to liberate one's intellectual soul from the prison of the body. A dualistic conception of the human being cannot do justice to a halakhic way of life. The Halakhah, which places such an emphasis on the performance of mitzvot, provides a different understanding of humanity. Halakhah speaks to the human will and gives primacy to action. It affirms the total person, both body and soul. R. Soloveitchik illustrates this integrative picture in the midrashic story that recalls how Moses wins his argument against the angels, who want the Torah to remain in heaven. Moses prevails by demonstrating that Torah was meant for human beings, who must cope with the daily struggles of everyday earthly existence.

> R. Joshua b. Levi also said: When Moses ascended on high, the ministering angels spake before the Holy One, blessed be He, "Sovereign of the Universe! What business has one born of woman amongst us?" "He has come to receive the Torah," answered He to them. Said they to Him, "That secret treasure, which has been hidden by Thee for nine hundred and seventy-four

generations before the world was created. Thou desirest to give to flesh and blood! *What is man, that thou are mindful of him, and the son of man, that thou visitest him? O Lord our God, How excellent is thy name in all the earth! Who hast set thy glory* [the Torah] *upon the Heavens!"* "Return them an answer," bade the Holy One, blessed be He, to Moses. . . . He [then] spake before Him, "Sovereign of the Universe! The Torah which Thou givest me, what is written therein? *I am the Lord thy God, which brought thee out of the Land of Egypt."* Said he to them [the angels], "Did ye go down to Egypt; were ye enslaved to Pharaoh: why then should the Torah be yours? Again what is written therein? *Thou shalt have none other gods:* do ye dwell among peoples that engage in idol worship? Again what is written therein? *Remember the Sabbath day, to keep it holy:* do ye then perform work, that ye need to rest? Again what is written therein? *Thou shalt not take [tissa] [the name . . . in vain]:* is there any business [*massa*] dealings among you? Again what is written therein? *Honour thy father and thy mother:* have ye fathers and mothers? Again what is written therein? *Thou shalt not murder. Thou shalt not commit adultery. Thou shalt not steal.* Is there jealousy among you? Is the Evil Tempter among you? Straightway they conceded [right] to the Holy One, blessed be He. (*b. Shabbat* 88b–89a)

R. Soloveitchik explains this midrash as follows:

God does not wish to hand over His Torah to the ministering angels, the denizens of a transcendent world. Rather, he handed over His Torah to Moses, who brought it down to the earth and caused it to dwell among human beings, "who reside in darkness and deep gloom." (Ps. 107:10) The earth and bodily life are the very ground of halakhic reality. Only against the concrete, empirical backdrop of this world can Torah be implemented; angels, who neither eat nor drink, who neither quarrel with one another nor are envious of one another, are not worthy and fit for the receiving of the Torah. (1983: 33–34)

THE FINITE WORLD: TWO PERSPECTIVES

Homo religiosus finds significance when life is wholly infused by eternity. For him, to feel at home in finitude represents a revolt against Divinity; to love temporal existence with a total passion is to fall into the trap of atheism. To believe in a transcendental, eternal God is to see in human history and in humankind's finite existence a blemish, a profoundly incomplete fragment.

For halakhic man, by contrast, spirituality does not consist in liberation from the chains of finitude. The revealed commandments comprise a total way of life that must be implemented within the social-political frameworks of human history. The God of mitzvah and Halakhah anchors halakhic man completely within the historical, and makes him understand that his true home lies within the temporal.

God is not in the true divine abode when separated from human history, when human sin, pride, arrogance, and brutality evict God from the world. When God is in heaven only, God is in exile. The true home of the divine is in this world, where God meets humankind in the domain of mitzvah, proclaiming, "Build for me a sanctuary on earth that I may dwell within it."

Halakhic man declares that the true home of the divine presence is in this world. The divine presence goes into exile according to the opinion of halakhic man when it departs from this world to the hidden and awesome transcendental realm. . . .

The universal *homo religiosus* proclaims: The lower yearns for the higher. But halakhic man, with his unique mode of understanding, declares: The higher longs and pines for the lower. (1983: 53, 39)

The spiritual world of halakhic man completely reverses the direction of the passion of *homo religiosus*. Halakhic man proclaims that the religious person does not need to obliterate finitude. Rather than embrace eternity, the religious person brings eternity into the realm of finitude. The world is not a pale image of eternity, but the true abode of the *Shekhinah*, the Divine Presence. This consciousness leads to a unique perception of redemption.

The ideal of halakhic man is the redemption of the world not via a higher world but via the world itself, via the adaptation of empirical reality to the ideal patterns of Halakhah. If a Jew lives in accordance with the Halakhah . . . then he shall find redemption. A lowly world is elevated through the Halakhah to the level of a divine world. (1983: 37–38)

R. Soloveitchik is aware of elements in the Judaic tradition that speak of eternal life and the soul's immortality, but he refuses to place these beliefs and concerns at the center of halakhic man's religious consciousness. As a traditional thinker who accepts the authority of the teachings of the past, he does not reject any of the Judaic dogmas such as resurrection of the dead, messianism, and immortality of the soul. They are all part of the teachings of the tradition. However, he selects from the tradition those mitzvot and dogmas necessary for constructing his ideal halakhic type. Thus, while R. Soloveitchik affirms the Jewish tradition in its entirety, this does not restrict him when he defines the central organizing and energizing principles in halakhic man's religious worldview.

One of the factors that make for interest in a traditional Jewish thinker is how that person gives importance to certain elements within the tradition, while allowing other principles to be present but not energizing and active. The traditional thinker respects everything, but celebrates and emphasizes what is particular and significant to his or her own religious context and situation. As Gershom Scholem noted, traditional thinkers do not eliminate dogmas in the tradition; they merely neutralize them.

This hermeneutical principle is crucial for making sense of thinkers like Maimonides and R. Soloveitchik. Failure to understand this method of selective emphasis has contributed to the disagreements among their interpreters. No one now denies that both Maimonides and R. Soloveitchik are Orthodox halakhists. However, there remains enormous room for disagreement as to the weight they gave to different aspects in the tradition. Regarding R. Soloveitchik, I suggest that his essay, although admitting belief in immortality and eschatological messianism, nevertheless locates the passion of halakhic man in a profoundly this-worldly attitude, in an appreciation of mitzvah that in no way requires the anticipation of reward and the blessedness of immortality. It is this earthbound concern for the "here and now" that characterizes halakhic man's experience of transcendence.

Halakhic man's sense of divinity is within the life of mitzvot, not in the redemptive drama of messianism, nor in the promise of a future life. In this light, it is highly instructive to contrast Kant and R. Soloveitchik with regard to their perception of morality and divinity. Kant proclaims that human reason, not God, must be the source of all truly moral imperatives. Yet, in order to ensure that moral action leads to happiness, Kant posits the existence of God and a future world, which guarantee that people will ultimately be rewarded for virtuous action. Halakhic man, by contrast, anchors all moral imperatives in the authority of God. Yet, he is prepared to say that the reward of mitzvah is the doing of the mitzvah itself. R. Soloveitchik's God thus keeps people joyfully anchored in the human-natural world.

Ironically, Kant's autonomous moral agent needs God in order to provide the promise of another world. Kant's morality breaks down unless he posits a transcendental realm that comprises humankind's final abode. Halakhic man, as portrayed by R. Soloveitchik, does not seek the quiet blissful existence that awaits Kant's moral agent.

> The Halakhah is not at all concerned with a transcendent world. The world to come is a tranquil, quiet world that is wholly good, wholly everlasting, and wholly eternal, wherein a man will receive the reward for the commandments which he performed in this world. However, the receiving of a reward is not a religious act; therefore, halakhic man prefers the real world to a transcendent existence because here, in this world, man is given the opportunity to create, act, accomplish, while there, in the world to come, he is powerless to change anything at all. (1983: 32)

For one whose total relationship to God is defined by a mitzvah consciousness, religious meaning thus lies only in performing a mitzvah. R. Soloveitchik cites many halakhic rulings to convince his readers that Judaism celebrates the joy of life and the full acceptance of human history. He relates how his grandfather insisted on paying strict attention to the principle of saving a life with regard to the fasting day on Yom Kippur. One must not take any risks when there is the slightest possibility of danger to life as a result of the fast.

> This law that *pikuah nefesh*, saving a life, overrides all the commandments and its far-reaching effects are indicative of the high value which the halakhic viewpoint attributes to one's earthly life—indeed they serve to confirm and nurture that value. Temporal life becomes transformed into eternal life, it becomes sanctified and elevated with eternal holiness. (1983: 35)

Because the priests were set apart and sanctified for the service of God, members of the priestly clan are not allowed to be in contact with death. Holiness is the antithesis to the melancholy and sadness evoked by tragedy. Joy is the mood required by one who is called upon to stand in God's presence. The great exemplars of Halakhah in R. Soloveitchik's tradition never visited cemeteries. Death is the antithesis to the world of mitzvah, which confirms human creativity, joy, and adequacy. Death defeats and levels, creating a sense of despair, futility, and nothingness. Meditating on death and eternity is antithetical to one who is blessed with a covenantal Halakhah that guides daily life.

> Many religions view the phenomenon of death as a positive spectacle, inasmuch as it highlights and sensitizes the religious consciousness and "sensibility." They, therefore, sanctify death and the grave because it is here that we find ourselves at the threshold of transcendence, at the portal of the world to come. Death is seen as a window filled with light, open to an exalted, supernal realm. Judaism, however, proclaims that coming into contact with the dead precipitates defilement. Judaism abhors death, organic decay, and

dissolution. It bids one to choose life and sanctify it. Authentic Judaism as reflected in halakhic thought sees in death a terrifying contradiction to the whole of religious life. Death negates the entire magnificent experience of halakhic man. (1983: 31)

HOMO RELIGIOSUS
AND MORAL APATHY

The desire to be liberated from the body and history has often created a religious consciousness that is immune or insensitive to the daily suffering of human beings. Why bother about disease, poverty, and physical oppression if one can find eternal peace? The longing for mystic union with God can become a deceptive way of numbing the religious spirit, preventing it from responding to human suffering and evil.

> *Homo religiosus*, his glance fixed upon the higher realms, forgets all too frequently the lower realms and becomes ensnared in the sins of ethical inconsistency and hypocrisy. See what many religions have done to this world on account of their yearning to break through the bonds of concrete reality and escape to the sphere of eternity. They have been so intoxicated by their dreams of an exalted supernal existence that they have failed to hear the cries of "them that dwell in houses of clay" (Job 91:4), the sighs of orphans, the groans of the destitute. (1983: 41)

Moral activism has often been understood as the antithesis to the quest for holiness and the longing for immortality. Not so in R. Soloveitchik's portrait of halakhic man's religious passion.

> Halakhic man is characterized by a powerful stiff-
> neckedness and stubbornness. He fights against
> life's evil and struggles relentlessly with the wicked
> kingdom and with all the hosts of iniquity in the cos-
> mos. (1983: 41)

This passion also infuses halakhic man's understanding of religious ritual. The whole of human life, not merely the synagogue, is the arena for worship of God.

> The primary difference between halakhic man and *homo religiosus* is that while the latter prefers the spirit to the body, the soul to its mortal frame, as the main actor in the religious drama, the former, as has been stated above, wishes to sanctify the physical-biological con-
> crete man as the hero and protagonist of religious life. Therefore, the whole notion of ritual assumes a special form in Judaism. The standard notion of ritual preva-
> lent among religious men—i.e., ritual as a nonrational religious act whose whole purpose is to lift man up from concrete reality to celestial realms—is totally for-
> eign to Judaism. . . . The Halakhah is not hermetically enclosed within the confines of cult sanctuaries but penetrates into every nook and cranny of life. The marketplace, the street, the factory, the house, the meeting place, the banquet hall, all constitute the backdrop for the religious life. The synagogue does not occupy a central place in Judaism. (1983: 94)

Halakhic man, as understood by R. Soloveitchik, is never far from the cries of the oppressed. His consciousness of God's commanding presence never allows him to forget that he is responsible and accountable for the social, economic, and political conditions

in human society. Covenantal halakhic consciousness is anchored in human history. Such consciousness is responsible to a God who seeks to be mirrored in the fullness of society. Halakhic man, therefore, never bifurcates moral passion from the life of ritual and worship. Endless arguments over ritual or ethics, as defining the essence of religious life, are totally alien to R. Soloveitchik's halakhic man.

Homo religiosus, who is primarily concerned with redemption from human finitude, perceives ritual as a preparation for a redeemed otherworldly existence. By emphasizing how infinity is brought into finitude, halakhic man sees mitzvot not as symbols of a transcendent realm, but as normative frameworks that enable human existence to embody the spirit of holiness. R. Soloveitchik's anthropocentric analysis of mitzvot totally reflects his central claim that halakhic man expresses his religious passion within the human world.

CREATION AS *IMITATIO DEI*

Halakhic man's self-confident spirit, in contrast to the passive resignation of *homo religiosus,* is brought into its sharpest focus in the final section of R. Soloveitchik's essay, where he discusses halakhic man's appreciation of and longing for creativity.

> The dream of creation is the central idea in the halakhic consciousness—the idea of the importance of man as a partner of the Almighty in the act of creation, man as creator of worlds. (1983: 99)

To convince his readers that a passionate desire for creativity is central to halakhic man, R. Soloveitchik turns to the biblical text. Like other interpreters of the halakhic tradition, R. Soloveitchik applies the centrality of halakhic practice to every statement of the Bible.

> The Halakhah sees the entire Torah as consisting of basic laws and halakhic principles. Even the Scriptural narratives serve the purpose of determining everlasting law. (1983: 99)

Scripture contains no normatively neutral metaphysical truths; every biblical statement about God and the world carries a whole series of behavioral consequences. In particular, the doctrine of creation is intended to invite and to challenge human beings to become God's partners in creation.

> Therefore, if the Torah spoke at length about the creation of the world and related to us the story of the making of heaven and earth and all their host, it did so not in order to reveal cosmogonic secrets and metaphysical mysteries but rather in order to teach *practical* Halakhah. The Scriptural portion of the creation narrative is a legal portion, in which are to be found basic, everlasting halakhic principles, just like the portion of *Kedoshim* (Lev. 19) or *Mishpatim* (Exod. 21). If the Torah then chose to relate to man the tale of creation, we may clearly derive one law from this manner of procedure— viz., that man is obliged to engage in creation and the renewal of the cosmos. (1983: 100–101)

Up to this point, other interpreters might go along with R. Soloveitchik. But he goes beyond them by relating this challenge to the concept of *imitatio Dei*. If God as Creator establishes the universe through the free activity of the divine will, and if God is not chained by causal necessity, then human beings created in

God's image are called upon to manifest these creative qualities of divinity in their own life.

This is a totally new way of interpreting the Judaic concept of *imitatio Dei*. The biblical admonition "And one should walk in His ways" was understood in the talmudic tradition simply as a commandment to imitate God's moral attributes. "Even as God is called gracious, so be you gracious; even as He is called merciful, so be you merciful; even as He is called holy, so be you holy" (*Sifre* 49; Maimonides, *M.T. Laws of Character Traits* 1:6). I know of no source within the rabbinic tradition stating that because God is the Creator of the universe, the human being must become a creator. Admittedly, the kabbalistic tradition does contain the notion that Jews affect a cosmic renewal and repair the splits present in the cosmos through the performance of mitzvot. But it is a bold step to suggest from this that human beings involved in science and technology are imitating God's role as Creator.

In R. Soloveitchik's essay, God's creativity is a motif infusing the entire normative halakhic tradition. Scientific curiosity and the desire to bring order and control into the cosmos are grounded, according to R. Soloveitchik, in the Judaic impulse to imitate God. The creation of the cosmos was not a unique act of divinity, but a paradigmatic process, initiated by God, to be completed by human beings. Thus the recitation of the *kiddush* prayer on Friday night, which proclaims God as Creator of the world, is understood by R. Soloveitchik as an invitation to human beings to become partners with God in the drama of creation.

> When a Jew on the Sabbath eve recites the *kiddush*, the sanctification over the wine, he testifies not only to the existence of a Creator but also to man's obligation to become a partner with the Almighty in the continuation and perfection of His creation. Just as the Almighty constantly refined and improved the realm of

existence during the six days of creation, so must man complete that creation and transform the domain of chaos and void into a prefect and beautiful reality. (1983: 105–6)

Likewise, R. Soloveitchik utilizes kabbalistic ideas suggesting that God created an imperfect world, in which chaos seeks to break into the orderly patterns of being. Humankind's task is then to build barriers against chaos and to extend the realm of order and structure to all of reality, both natural and historical.

When God created the world, He provided an opportunity for the work of His hands—man—to participate in His creation. The Creator, as it were, impaired reality in order that mortal man could repair its flaws and perfect it. (1983: 101)

R. Soloveitchik is not disturbed by the bold efforts of modern science to extend the boundaries of human knowledge. This very yearning, he believes, is in harmony with the biblical teachings of God as Creator of the universe. According to R. Soloveitchik, the contrast between the Jewish doctrine of creation and the Aristotelian belief that the universe has existed from all eternity must be understood in terms of the different normative perspectives and challenges they pose. Since the Greeks ascribed greater reality to whatever is unchanging and uncreated, they saw human excellence not in the active transformation of the world, but in the philosophical contemplation of eternal verities. Judaism emphasizes the unfolding of the principle of will and energy, the dynamic longing for shaping, transforming, and controlling the world.

The whole concept of creation never really took hold in Greek philosophy. As a result of this, Greek philosophy had no room for the true creative act. . . . The pure, first form does not create; therefore, man is not obliged to create. . . . Neither the intellectual virtues of Aristotelian ethics nor the aspiration for the contemplative life (*Bios theoretikos*) are in any way equivalent with the yearning for creation that has so entirely seized hold of the Jewish imagination. (1983: 133)

The halakhic personality's longing to create is expressed not only in the desire to change the world, but equally, and perhaps even to a greater extent, in the yearning to complete the creation of one's individual being by unfolding one's own unique individual capacities. By emphasizing the notion of God as Creator, Judaism introduced the significance of self-creation as a profound ethical ideal.

The most fundamental principle of all is that man must create himself. It is this idea that Judaism introduced into the world. (1983: 109)

The belief that God created the world is translated into a normative challenge to live a heroic existence where freedom replaces necessity, where hopefulness and confidence guide one's perception of the future. Halakhic man does not live a melancholy life waiting to be liberated from the prison of human sin and the human body. It is not grace alone that liberates halakhic man, but rather, the sense that God calls on him to build a free and spontaneous existence.

PROVIDENCE AND SELF-CREATION

R. Soloveitchik's normative interpretation of metaphysical doctrines is further exemplified by his discussion of providence. Among medieval philosophers, the controversy over divine providence was related to the already mentioned conflict between the Greek assertion that the universe is eternal and the Jewish belief in creation. For Aristotle, God is the source of nature's ordered necessary patterns. The Aristotelian God does not get involved in any individual events, whether in nature or in human history. The Jewish doctrine of creation, on the other hand, depicts a free, spontaneous God, who is able to break into the ordered patterns of nature and respond to the needs of the single human individual. Judaism's Creator God is able to establish an intimate relationship with a particular human community and promises to assist it in history, as long as it remains loyal to God's covenantal norms. The impersonal Aristotelian God ensures only general providence, which guarantees merely the continued existence of the human species, mediated through the laws of nature. The personal God of the Bible can also ensure the particular providence of human individuals, mediated through the covenantal drama of the Jewish community in history.

From R. Soloveitchik's halakhic functional perspective, however, the difference between Aristotelian and Judaic teachings of providence is not primarily metaphysical. Rather, it is a normative conflict between a static worldview, which absorbs the individual within the framework of the universal, and a dynamic one, which presents the human individual with a challenge of moving from mere species existence to an individual life defined by freedom, will, and the yearning for individual self-realization. R. Soloveitchik thus reformulates the controversy in existentialist categories, such that the medieval philosophers would hardly recognize their original dispute.

Man, at times, exists solely by virtue of the species, by virtue of the fact that he was born a member of that species, and its general form is engraved upon him. . . . His soul, his spirit, his entire being, all are grounded in the realm of the universal. His roots lie deep in the soil of faceless mediocrity; his growth takes place solely within the public domain. He has no stature of his own, no original, individual, personal profile. He has never created anything. . . . He is wholly under the influence of other people and their views. . . . This is man as the random example of the biological species. But there is another man, one who does not require the assistance of others, who does not need the support of the species to legitimate his existence. . . . His life is replete with creation and renewal, cognition and profound understanding. . . . He does not simply abandon himself to the rule of the species but blazes his own individual trail. Moreover, he, as an individual, influences the many. . . . This is the man of God. (1983: 126–28)

From R. Soloveitchik's perspective, Maimonides' teaching on providence challenges the individual to discover his or her uniqueness and individuality. Does one shape one's own private domain and create one's own individual autobiography, filled with spontaneity, freedom, and creativity? Or does one remain dominated by the realm of mere necessity? Ultimately, this is an open question decided by the individual's existential choices. Whether any given human individual takes advantage of the opportunity provided by this understanding of individual providence is up to himself or herself. It is possible for human beings to live their lives largely on the species level, like animals. To pass beyond that level, the individual must deliberately choose action and creation.

Species man or man of God—this is the alternative which the Almighty placed before man. If he proves worthy, then he becomes a man of God in all the splendor of his individual existence that cleaves to absolute infinity and the glorious "divine overflow." If he proves unworthy, then he ends up as one mere random example of the biological species, a turbid and blurred image of universal existence. (1983: 125–26)

Being worthy or unworthy, for R. Soloveitchik, is not a gift of grace; it is not God's miraculous interference that transforms a human being from one form of existence to another. Rather, the change is initiated by the freedom and will of the particular human individual. The doctrine of individual providence is then not an assertion about God's relationship to humankind, but a commandment to be realized by the individual.

Man is obliged to broaden the scope and strengthen the intensity of the individual providence that watches over him. Everything is dependent on him; it is all in his hands. When a person creates himself, ceases to be a mere species man, and becomes a man of God, then he has fulfilled that commandment which is implicit in the principle of providence. (1983: 128)

THE PROPHET AS
PARADIGM OF HUMAN FREEDOM

The normative paradigm of the individual who has totally renounced mere species life, and whose life is guided by the free spontaneous spirit of the person of God, is the prophet.

> The most exalted creation of all is the personality of
> the prophet. Each man is obligated to give new life to
> his own being by modeling his personality upon the
> image of the prophet; he must carry through his own
> self-creation until he actualizes the idea of prophecy.
> (1983: 128)

R. Soloveitchik's account of prophecy, like his discussion of
creation and providence, radically changes the focus of the medieval debate. The medieval discussions of prophecy revolved
around the nature of the prophet and the conditions necessary for
the prophet to receive the gracious outpouring of God. The medievals were concerned with the status of prophecy: is it a miraculous gift of God to a chosen human being, or rather, the fullest
development of the natural intellectual and moral excellence with
which any human being is potentially endowed at birth? To what
degree does the prophet gain access to metaphysical truths not
available to the philosopher? Does the unique status of the prophet
lie in cognitive capacities, in the truth he or she brings to human
beings, or does that unique status lie in promulgating a divine
law? Is prophecy *sui generis*, distinct from any other perfection
available to human beings, or must we understand the uniqueness
of prophecy within the categories of political statesmanship and
leadership?

R. Soloveitchik is fully aware that the outpouring of the
spirit, "the divine overflow is dependent upon heavenly grace"
(1983: 130). Prophecy, for R. Soloveitchik, is not a natural category. Indeed, he hints in his essay that he would identify with those
medievals who regarded prophecy as a gift of divine grace, not with
those who saw it as a natural category. But this is by no means the
focus of his discussion. He is interested in the personality of the
prophet, not in the phenomenon of prophecy. He is not concerned

89

with what metaphysical claims might be needed to justify the whole idea of prophecy.

Likewise, R. Soloveitchik is totally uninterested in the medieval discussion of the ideal geographical climate for prophecy, in the arguments of Halevi and Nachmanides, that the unique ontological status of the Land of Israel provides the conditions for prophecy. Nor is he concerned whether prophecy is a unique capacity found only among Jews in Israel or a spiritual capacity available to all humanity. R. Soloveitchik is interested in the prophet as a paradigm inspiring individuals to energize their full unique capacities. He is not concerned with what God does in prophecy, but with what individuals can become through appropriating the norm of prophecy in their own personal development.

The Talmud taught that the scholar replaced the prophet after the destruction of the Temple. Indeed, the halakhic tradition has forsaken the idea of ongoing revelation—rabbinic sages never begin their Torah discourse by announcing that the word of God burns within them. Nevertheless, R. Soloveitchik found it necessary to reintroduce the personality of the prophet into his description of halakhic man. He is not interested in revelatory grace, but rather, in the anthropological significance of prophecy for contemporary human beings. How does the prophetic personality speak to a human condition that must cope with conformism, anomie, and mediocrity?

R. Soloveitchik gives a normative activist thrust to the Judaic teaching of prophecy. The prophet is the paradigm of freedom. The prophet represents the telos toward which creative humankind must aspire. The prophet is the epitome of one who breaks the chains of necessity and shapes an identity totally through his or her own creative powers.

The prophet creates his own personality, fashions within himself a new "I" awareness and a different mode of spiritual existence, snaps the chains of self-identity that had linked him to the "I" of old—to man who was just a random example of the species, who "walk[ed] in the darkness of the times"—and turns into a man of God, his mind "bound beneath the [celestial] throne." (1983: 130)

For R. Soloveitchik, the prophet is the symbol of the truly free human being, embodying Kierkegaard's longing to be the single one, reflecting Nietzsche's claim that "the goal of mankind cannot lie at the close of history but in its highest examples."

Complete freedom belongs only to the prophet, the man of God. The man who is a mere random example of the species, on the other hand, is wholly under the rule of the scientific lawfulness of existence. Between this species man and the man of God, between necessity and freedom, is the middle range in which most people find themselves. Some ascend in the direction of complete freedom; others descend in the direction of complete servitude. (1983: 135)

R. Soloveitchik's conception of creation, providence, and prophecy mirrors a healthy-minded, self-confident spirit. The model of God as Creator energizes the human will and presents a universe that awaits halakhic man's creative imprint. Such a healthy-minded, activist spirit is antithetical to *homo religiosus*, who yearns for divine grace and liberation from human finitude.

SELF-RENEWAL, SIN, AND ATONEMENT

The self-reliant spirit flourishes in a world in which God invites the human being to become a partner in creation. But what happens when human adequacy backfires? When the optimistic spirit is choked by repeated failures and disappointments? When one fails to live up to the normative obligations of the covenant? When one encounters not the joy of creativity but the painful hollowness of self-defilement through sin and wrongdoing?

The increasing sense of guilt that derives from repeated sin does not energize the will, but leads instead to a sense of resignation and helplessness. It is in such moments that the human being would naturally seek some external support, some movement from the divine other toward himself or herself. Our faith in our human creative capacities can be paralyzed by the tormenting pain of so much human failure and guilt. If there is a human need for grace, it should be reflected on such occasions. Nevertheless, it is in the context of human sin that R. Soloveitchik heightens the contrast between halakhic man's self-reliant spirit and the yearning for grace that characterizes *homo religiosus.*

> Here there comes to the fore the primary difference be-
> tween the concept of repentance in Halakhah and the
> concept of repentance held by *homo religiosus.* The latter
> views repentance only from the perspective of atone-
> ment, only as a guard against punishment, as an empty
> regret which does not create anything, does not bring
> into being anything new. A deep melancholy afflicts his
> spirit. He mourns for the yesterdays that are irretrievably
> past, the times that have long since sunk into the abyss of
> oblivion, the deeds that have vanished like shadows, facts
> that he will never be able to change. Therefore, for *homo
> religiosus,* repentance is a wholly miraculous phenomenon

made possible by the endless grace of the Almighty. But such is not the case with halakhic man! Halakhic man does not indulge in weeping and despair, does not lacerate his flesh or flail away at himself. He does not afflict himself with penitential rites and forgoes all mortification of body and soul. Halakhic man is engaged in self-creation, in creating a new "I." (1983: 113)

R. Soloveitchik makes an important distinction between *teshuvah* (repentance) as self-creation and *teshuvah* as atonement (*kapparah*). In atonement, one seeks the gracious forgiveness of God. A religious person cannot begin a new life before being assured that sin has not created a permanent alienation from God. Yet this yearning for atonement, which features prominently in R. Soloveitchik's oral discourses on *teshuvah*, as well as in many passages of the Bible and the Talmud, is given peripheral significance in *Halakhic Man*. Here, he emphasizes how repentance flows from the individual's ability to forge a new identity.

> Atonement, however, is only a peripheral aspect of repentance. Its central aspect is the termination of a negative personality, the sinner's divesting himself of his status as a *rasha*—indeed, the total obliteration of that status. . . . The desire to be another person, to be different than I am now, is the central motif of repentance. Man cancels the law of identity and continuity which prevails in the "I" awareness by engaging in the wondrous, creative act of repentance. A person is creative; he was endowed with the power to create at his very inception. (1983: 112–13)

The elaborate demands of halakhic Judaism would have crushed human freedom and spontaneity if one experienced human sinfulness as a crushing experience of guilt and self-loathing due to one's estrangement from God. The propensity for human failure and weakness does not at all diminish the spirit of self-confidence nurtured by the Judaic tradition. The vitality of halakhic Judaism hangs on its permanent belief in the human capacity for self-renewal. For R. Soloveitchik, halakhic man never loses faith in the human capacity to recreate and reshape the significance of his past.

"The path to teshuvah is never closed" (see Maimonides, *M.T. Laws of Teshuvah* 3:14). The past does not determine the future. New possibilities are always open for the human spirit. Even at the last moment of life, one can give a new significance to one's entire existence. Nothing stands in the way of *teshuvah*. This is the essential spirit that infuses the life of halakhic man.

> When he finds himself in a situation of sin, he takes advantage of his creative capacity, returns to God, and becomes a creator and self-fashioner. Man, through repentance, creates himself, his own "I." (1983: 113)

In this ability to transform even sin into an occasion for renewed self-creation, R. Soloveitchik expresses halakhic man's final repudiation of the need for divine grace. *Homo religiosus,* who seeks redemption from this world, stands condemned before God in his sinfulness. His only hope is to wait for God's atoning grace. Halakhic man does not revel in guilt, in self-mortification. Sin does not turn his eyes helplessly heavenwards, but rather, spurs him to look intensively into his own life, into his own past, into the condition that created his tendency to fail. *Teshuvah* is a call to renewal, not to resignation.

SELF-CREATION AS A RELIGIOUS IDEAL

R. Soloveitchik's teaching on creation, with its emphasis on freedom and self-creation, is central for understanding his approach to
teshuvah. Creation introduces the principle of will—the call upon
man to self-creation. Providence provides a way to liberate the individual from the faceless mediocrity of the masses. It shows the
importance of distinguishing between the species life of animals
and the sacredness of a single human life. Halakhic appreciation of
community must accommodate the yearning for individual self-
realization. To be holy, to imitate God, one must strive for uniqueness and individuality. The path to freedom and uniqueness, the
liberation from social conformism, is a long and arduous struggle.

Only a few individuals can completely realize the telos of the
Halakhah. But it is these singular individuals—prophets or Torah
scholars—who serve as exemplars of that to which the community
should aspire. Although covenantal Halakhah never distinguished
between the elite and the masses with regard to normative practice,
it nevertheless encouraged the growth of individual human excellence, which, for R. Soloveitchik, means freedom and creativity.
Without the paradigm of the prophet, who acts as a catalyst urging
individuals to strive for uniqueness, the Halakhah would be reduced to a mediocre and soulless regimen. R. Soloveitchik thus discerns a spiritual process that moves from creation through *teshuvah*
and providence to prophecy.

> In sum, the task of creation with which man is charged
> is, according to the Halakhah, a triple performance;
> it finds its expression in the capacity to perform *teshu-*
> *vah,* to repent, continues to unfold in *hashgahah,*
> the unique providence which is bestowed upon the
> unique individual, and achieves its final and ultimate

95

realization in the reality of prophecy and the personality of the prophet. . . .

When God apportioned some of His glory to mortal
man and bestowed upon him the power of creation, He
grounded this creative power in man's will. The will
outwits the structured lawfulness of the species; it creates a new, free mode of being in man, one which is not
enslaved by the rule of the structured lawfulness of the
universal. . . . The will is the source of repentance,
providence, prophecy, and the freedom of the spirit.
(1983: 130–31, 137)

To travel on the road of Halakhah, to appreciate the prophet
as a paradigm of excellence, to accept with joy the challenge to recreate the world, to bring order into chaos on both the personal and the
collective levels, one must never see human limitations as signs of sinfulness and insignificance. The God who finds the true divine home
in the finite human world will never reject and condemn someone for
the sinful failure to live up to the normative demands of Halakhah.
The God whose will is mediated through the mitzvot, the God
whose own destiny is bound in a covenant with the living community of Israel, will never undermine the foundations of the covenant
by losing faith in the creative capacities of human beings.

R. Soloveitchik's loyalty and commitment to his family's halakhic worldview did not prevent him from using the "wisdom of
the nations" to clarify the inner world of the traditional halakhic
personality. His distinctive way of weaving Western existentialist
motifs into his presentation of the halakhic tradition is a marvelous
example of Leo Strauss's insight that "genuine fidelity to a tradition is not the same as literalist traditionalism."

4

THE LONELY MAN OF FAITH

THE SELF-CONFIDENT SPIRIT that pervades *Halakhic Man* seems entirely absent from R. Soloveitchik's second major theological essay, "The Lonely Man of Faith." Halakhic man was characterized by his unique perception of God's revelatory law, by the joy that he experiences both in the study of Torah and in the observance of mitzvot, by his passionate, creative longing to be engaged in transforming the world. The religious anthropology in "The Lonely Man of Faith" seems closer to *homo religiosus* than to the ideal halakhic personality explored in the previous two chapters.

In "The Lonely Man of Faith," unlike *Halakhic Man*, R. Soloveitchik is deeply concerned with the religious individual's longing for redemption. The lonely man of faith encounters frequent defeat and resignation. What happened to the confident and healthy-minded Judaic spirit that R. Soloveitchik depicted in such a striking way in *Halakhic Man?*

Is the discrepancy to be explained simply by distinguishing between the historical contexts in which the respective essays were written? One could argue that since *Halakhic Man* was written during a period of optimism about scientific advance, R. Soloveitchik tried to bring the halakhic personality into the modern world by emphasizing its cognitive, self-confident, and activist spirit. After World War II, however, and certainly by the 1960s, Western civilization's sense of faith in itself was on the wane. The problematic complexities of human life and society had reasserted themselves as strongly as ever. There was a lack of optimistic belief that science and technology would solve all human dilemmas. Certainly, there are echoes of the contemporary spirit of Western society in both essays. But can the difference between them be attributed solely to the change in the external ambience between two generations?

David Singer and Moshe Sokol interpret the discrepancy between *Halakhic Man* and "The Lonely Man of Faith" as a profound inner conflict within R. Soloveitchik himself. He is, they claim, a torn personality. On the one hand, he is loyal to the tradition of his father and grandfather, which emphasized study, pure emotional detachment, and stoic indifference, celebrating the cerebral aspects of the human personality. On the other hand, there is R. Soloveitchik the Hasid, the emotionally involved person who realizes that the intellect cannot exhaust the religious life, that all dimensions of the human psyche must play their role in building a religious consciousness.

The Hasid and the Brisker halakhist in R. Soloveitchik struggle constantly with each other, according to Singer and Sokol. Consequently, whereas the message of *Halakhic Man* is to use your mind, that of "The Lonely Man of Faith" is to trust your feelings. When R. Soloveitchik speaks of the necessity of conflict, contradiction, and struggle, when he emphasizes the inner life of the religious personality and not pure learning and formal behavior, he is giving expression to the emotional dimensions of his own conflict-ridden personality.

Most certainly, there is a side of Soloveitchik that responds with total enthusiasm to his familial-cultural
heritage of undiluted intellectualism, of a fierce
commitment to mind as the one sure guide to truth.
Soloveitchik the Litvak is no figment of the imagination; he does exist. But there is yet another side to
Soloveitchik, and this side is incapable of endorsing
what the Litvak in him affirms. Litvak intellectualism
may speak to Soloveitchik's mind, but it ignores the reality of what he *feels*—feelings so strong that they eventually burst through the dam in "The Lonely Man of
Faith." . . .

As for "The Lonely Man of Faith," it depicts religious life as painfully wrenching at every turn; the
"knight of faith," according to Soloveitchik, is ontologically torn, existentially lonely, and engaged in
repetitive sacrificial gestures. . . . All in all, Soloveitchik's emphasis on the painful nature of religious experience is clear-cut. What is so obvious is that this
stress reflects the personal burden of pain which he
carries as an individual torn between the claims of Litvak intellectualism on the one side and a Hasidic-like
affirmation of the emotions on the other.[7]

Lawrence Kaplan, a lifelong devoted student of R. Soloveitchik and the translator of *Halakhic Man,* offers a quite different explanation of the contrast between the Soloveitchik of "The
Lonely Man of Faith" and the Soloveitchik of *Ish ha-Halakhah*
(*Halakhic Man*) in light of the different audiences to whom they
are addressed. According to Kaplan, R. Soloveitchik's deepest religious convictions are revealed only in his Hebrew writings, such

---

[7]Singer and Sokol, "Joseph Soloveitchik," 258, 260.

as *Halakhic Man*. The English essays, such as "The Lonely Man of Faith," were addressed to a wider audience and reflect the full ambivalence of R. Soloveitchik's attitude toward Western civilization. R. Soloveitchik is concerned with the hubris so characteristic of modern humanity, the celebration of technology and the exaggerated self-confidence that reduce religion to functional utilitarian categories. As much as he appreciates modernity, R. Soloveitchik believes it is necessary to balance Western society's self-confident spirit with a passionate faith experience deeply grounded in resignation, sacrifice, and humility. Consequently, his English essays, such as "The Lonely Man of Faith," dwell upon the conflict between the assertive and self-negating features of religious consciousness in all its stark dimensions. In his Hebrew writings, by contrast, R. Soloveitchik shows how Judaism can resolve the conflict by creating a harmonious religious personality, since he believes that Halakhah and Torah provide a sufficient protection from the hubris and arrogance of the Western personality.

> In his English essays, the ideal religious personality is not "the harmonious individual . . . but the torn soul and the shattered spirit." The man of faith is a deeply divided personality, "involved in an unresolvable contradiction, an insoluble dialectic . . . caught like Abraham's ram in a thicket of antinomies and dichotomies." The rational religious consciousness and the revealed religious consciousness give rise to such opposite polar qualities as majesty and humility, creativity and sacrifice, triumph and defeat, freedom and compulsion. The tension between these qualities is ultimate and not to be transcended. . . .
>
> In his Hebrew essays, however, the image of the ideal religious personality is one of a balanced, integrated

individual. . . . Harmony, not tension and conflict, is then, the final word, the ultimate goal, though that harmony arises out of tension and conflict.[8]

The psychological reductionism of Singer and Sokol does not do justice to the intellectual depth and subtle complexity of R. Soloveitchik's writings. Nor does Kaplan's distinction between R. Soloveitchik's writings in Hebrew and his writings in English provide an explanation, since it presumes that the former were written for Jews firmly rooted in the Orthodox tradition, the latter for Jews attracted by assimilation to modernity. In fact, however, R. Soloveitchik's Hebrew writings were not written for traditional Jews. The essay "Ish ha-Halakhah" ("Halakhic Man") first appeared in the journal *Talpioth*, which was not read necessarily by traditional yeshivah students. Nor was "Ma Dodekh Mi-dod," his other Hebrew-language essay on halakhic phenomenology, published in a traditional magazine, but rather in *Ha-Doar*, which was read by secular Hebraists. On the other hand, the English essay "The Lonely Man of Faith" was published in *Tradition*, a magazine read primarily by an Orthodox audience. The difference in style between English and Hebrew is also in no way a sufficient basis to evaluate his writings.

THE UNIVERSAL DIMENSIONS OF THE LONELY MAN OF FAITH

How, then, does one make sense of the obvious difference between the religious phenomenology of "The Lonely Man of Faith" and

---

[8]Lawrence Kaplan, "Models of the Ideal Religious Man in Rabbi Soloveitchik's Thought" (in Hebrew), *Jerusalem Studies in Jewish Thought* 4, nos. 3–4 (1984–1985): 337–39.

Halakhic Man? In contrast to what I assumed in my book
A Living Covenant, where I treated R. Soloveitchik's "The Lonely
Man of Faith" as a purely Judaic type, I now believe that "The
Lonely Man of Faith" is not a phenomenology of the Judaic experience alone. R. Soloveitchik's "lonely man" is not peculiar to the
traditional Jewish community; he also surfaces within other faith
communities that emphasize revelation and a personal God. The
fundamental difference between the two essays lies in the fact that
the point of departure for *Halakhic Man* is the normative experience within Judaism. One consequence is the strong apologetic
motif in *Halakhic Man.* There is special pleading. R. Soloveitchik
feels an urgent need to present this halakhic personality in the best
light, as a compelling figure projecting the image of a human type
that is responsive to the new spirit of self-creativity, autonomy, and
dignity so prevalent in the nineteenth and twentieth centuries. In
"The Lonely Man of Faith," by contrast, the focus is not the defense of a maligned tradition, but rather, the clarification of the existential condition of the Western man of faith, who participates in
a civilization that is drunk with its ever growing sense of technological power and mastery. R. Soloveitchik seeks to explain the faith
of a modern individual who often feels alien and misunderstood in
a world that celebrates technological success, scientific achievements, and total confidence in human adequacy.

In order to clarify the existential condition of loneliness, R.
Soloveitchik uses biblical and halakhic material to illuminate the
universal dilemma of the man of faith. Talmudic and midrashic literature, Maimonides and Nachmanides—all these Jewish sources
are brought into discussion with Kant, Kierkegaard, and other
writers who do not speak out of the halakhic tradition. A deep pre-
supposition appears to lie underneath R. Soloveitchik's "The
Lonely Man of Faith," as also beneath his *Halakhic Mind:* there is
a universal condition that is constitutive of the faith experience in
all revelatory traditions. This common ground enables R. Soloveit-

chik to create a discussion between the Jewish and non-Jewish traditions.

By examining R. Soloveitchik's argument, I will show that in "The Lonely Man of Faith" the Jewish tradition illustrates a universal experiential condition shared by all human beings who are touched by the urgent need for an in-depth faith experience, which R. Soloveitchik calls the covenantal moment of faith. "The Lonely Man of Faith" opens with this assertion: "I am mainly interested in contemporary man of faith, who is, due to his peculiar position in our secular society, lonely in a special way" (1965: 8). Having thus stated his concern about the contemporary man of faith, not just halakhic man, R. Soloveitchik describes himself as sharing in the loneliness of Western men of faith.

> What can a man of faith, like myself, living by a doctrine which has no technical potential, by a law which cannot be tested in the laboratory, steadfast to his loyalty to an eschatological vision whose fulfillment cannot be predicted with any degree of probability, let alone certainty, even by the most complex, advanced mathematical calculation—what can such a man say to a functional utilitarian society which is *saeculum*-oriented and whose practical reasons of the mind have long ago supplanted the sensitive reasons of the heart? (1965: 8)

There is something essential to this posture of loneliness, which is not a particular psychological quirk of Jews or of individuals like R. Soloveitchik, but is deeply rooted in a religious person's understanding of his or her place in the universe. Of course, the categories that R. Soloveitchik uses to clarify this condition of loneliness are drawn from his own scriptural and theological tradition. As a man of faith, he interprets his personal condition of loneliness within his own religious matrix, rather than abandoning the framework of his own tradition and using psychological or empirical categories to explain his condition.

THE TWO HUMAN TYPES FOUND
IN THE CREATION STORY

Whereas in *Halakhic Man* the means for shaping R. Soloveitchik's religious anthropology are drawn exclusively from the halakhic framework, in "The Lonely Man of Faith" his discussion starts not with Halakhah but with the biblical story of creation. It is important to notice the distinction between R. Soloveitchik's use of the terms "biblical" and "halakhic"; much confusion results when they are treated as if they were identical. By "halakhic," he understands the way Judaism gave a particular form to a universal biblical worldview. In beginning with the story of creation, he sets a universal frame of reference for understanding the faith experience shared by all lonely men of faith whose self-understanding is drawn from biblical theistic conceptions.

For medieval Jewish thinkers, the creation story is the ground for the belief in miracles (Maimonides), or anticipates how God becomes involved in the life of particular communities (Rashi and Judah Halevi). R. Soloveitchik, however, starts his analysis from the description of the creation of male and female. The two creation stories found at the beginning of Genesis then form a metahistorical framework for illuminating the human condition, inasmuch as they variously characterize the role that God assigned to human beings in the scheme of creation. The first story—the seven days of creation—describes the creation of man and woman together. In the second story, in contrast, they meet in a dramatic encounter absent from the first. Here Adam, created alone, in vain seeks company among the animals, until God removes his loneliness by creating woman as his helpmate.

To modern biblical scholars, this difference between the two stories is interesting because it reflects the different views of two distinct authors. For R. Soloveitchik, a traditional Orthodox Jew who believes in the unitary authorship of the Bible, it reflects two different ways that human beings can understand themselves. He uses it to depict two different "Adams," that is, two models of how the individual understands himself or herself, what needs he or she brings to human relationships, the type of community that each of them builds, and how these human dynamics reflect two distinct modes of manifestation of God, who is called Elohim in the first creation story and by the Tetragrammaton in the second. These two models of the human individual, interpersonal relationship, community, and the God-experience form two different conceptual frameworks through which human beings understand their roles in relation to God and nature.

The first type, which R. Soloveitchik calls "Adam the first," sees the world as an object to be mastered. Adam the first believes that the human being's task is to impose order upon chaos and to provide the means for his best survival within a hostile or indifferent nature. He sees the essential human quest in overcoming vulnerability to nature, which crushes human beings with afflictions such as epidemics and infant mortality. The growth of science and technology provides him with a sense of dignity. To cope with illness, poverty, and homelessness in a mute, indifferent world gives him a sense of worth and esteem. "Be fruitful and multiply, replenish the earth and subdue it, and have dominion . . . over every living thing that moves on the earth" (Gen. 1:28).

Adam the first does not perceive the challenge of life within internal human existential categories. The problem is not human authenticity, love, or relationship. The interpersonal in no way defines the frame of reference for what is ultimate and significant in life.

Through the unleashing of energy and power, Adam the

first senses his humanity. The human relationships that he builds, therefore, grow also from this desire to escape from helplessness. He forms a community of interests, defined by the need to master an external world, in which the need to overcome poverty, hunger, and weakness cements human beings together in a cooperative effort.

R. Soloveitchik calls this form of community a work community, which defines its relational posture via the struggle to achieve dignity and power. It is like a family that is too poor to have time to deal with in-depth psychological issues of boredom and anomie, emptiness and meaninglessness. They have no sense of purposelessness.

R. Soloveitchik's distinction may be illustrated by the story of a young rabbi who, when informing his immigrant parents of his decision to leave his first pulpit, was asked if it was because they had not paid his salary. Although he told them that he was seeking deeper meaning, self-fulfillment, and new opportunities to express his own religious creativity, they could only translate his existentialist concerns into functional problems of economic survival. For the immigrant who had faced the indignity of poverty, of not being able to pay the rent and provide adequately for the children, that frame of reference filtered and colored the whole perception of what it meant to be a dignified human being.

Nor does the God of Adam the first meet him in an intimate relational framework. Adam the first is not receptive to a God who would choose an intensive relation to humanity. As long as he asks only functional questions, as long as his frame of reference is mastery, his God-consciousness is of Elohim, the God of majesty and power. Intensity of love and intimacy with the Godhead cannot become the concern until there is a fundamental shift in the interpersonal framework, which R. Soloveitchik finds in "Adam the second," for whom "it is not good to be alone" (1965: 33).

The revelatory mode in which God appears in deep, intimate

frameworks, the framework in which God addresses man in his singularity—this mode is possible only when the type of concerns that the human brings to self-definition changes. The human being must see nature not as an object to be mastered, but as a reality to be met in its qualitative richness. Nature here fascinates and creates puzzles as to why one is alive. How does one explain one's accidental qualities? How does one relate one's fleeting existence to something more permanent and anchored? How does one deal with the reality of finitude and death? How does one explain why there is a world and what is the purpose for human existence? How does one's own individual existence fit into a larger purposeful framework?

Here human beings seek to anchor their identity and their perception of life within a larger metaphysical picture. The world is not an object to be controlled, but a reality to be experienced with a sense of wonderment, puzzlement, and surprise. It is the qualitative framework of being, rather than the functional question, that Adam the second brings to nature.

When such an epistemological transformation occurs, so also the human self-definition changes. Human dignity is now seen in the quest for purpose, meaning, and relationship. One becomes aware of one's singularity, of one's otherness from nature. The work project does not suffice to define identity. Suddenly one senses one's aloneness. One realizes the incommensurability between self-consciousness and the objective world. One seeks to break out of this enormous sense of loneliness.

In seeking to discover purpose and significance, one likewise seeks a God who can address the human being and provide a frame of reference for total dedication and passion of love. One is not satisfied with knowing Elohim, the impersonal God of the cosmos; one seeks a God who has a personal name, the Tetragrammaton. It is this quest for relational intensity and intimacy with God that

R. Soloveitchik calls the faith commitment or the covenantal commitment.

DEFEAT AND REDEMPTION

These frames of reference become then the feature defining the personality of Adam the second. The human being whom you seek in this framework is equally single and unique. What you bring to the relationship is not a common goal to master helplessness and achieve dignity. Rather, you bring a quest to overcome loneliness, to achieve friendship, or, to use theological language, to achieve redemption. Redemption in this context is not an otherworldly yearning to be liberated from the body, but a desire to overcome the sense of loneliness that haunts those who experience their own uniqueness and singularity. Only with another human spirit, only through sharing common commitments, only through making room for the other in a relational context, does a new form of community emerge—the covenantal community.

> If Adam is to bring his quest for redemption to full re-alization, he must initiate action leading to the discovery of a companion who, even though as unique and singular as he, will master the art of communicating and, with him, form a community. However, this action, since it is part of the redemptive gesture, must also be sacrificial. The medium of attaining full redemption is, again, defeat. This new companionship is not attained through conquest, but through surrender and retreat. "And the eternal God caused an overpowering sleep to fall upon man." Adam was overpowered and defeated—and in defeat he found his companion. (1965: 26)

This religious yearning for redemption should in no way be identified with the quest for redemptive grace found in R. Soloveitchik's portrait of *homo religiosus* in *Halakhic Man*. It is important to note that R. Soloveitchik does not use the language of defeat and sacrifice only when man encounters God. Redemption is not here a theological category restricted to describing the posture of *homo religiosus* standing before God in passive resignation, overwhelmed by guilt, feeling totally unable to draw upon his own resources, and requiring grace in order to experience redemption. It is also a category reflected in the way human beings relate to each other.

R. Soloveitchik uses the notions of defeat and sacrifice as necessary characteristics of a new type of relationship between human beings, who know themselves to be unique, exclusive, and singular. It is the way in which the Kierkegaardian "single one" is able, instead of choosing loneliness as a permanent feature of life, to move beyond his or her exclusiveness to the other.

By speaking of defeat, R. Soloveitchik points to the antithesis to Adam the first, who regards power as the only form of dignity, who feels that he has a place in the world only to the degree to which he can master his environment. Here it is not objective and indifferent nature that sets the agenda, but the "other," the quest for relationship. In order to make room for the "other," there must then be a self-limiting, a giving up of control, an ability to live without power. Indeed, the ideal of control embraced by Adam the first destroys the possibility for an intense relational framework. The interpersonal now becomes the frame of reference that provides meaning, depth, and identity. To make room for a God who can address man, to make room for a God who could provide a normative challenge for man, R. Soloveitchik calls for defeat and sacrificial action, the posture that makes room for relational intensity.

R. Soloveitchik's use of the term "defeat" should not be

understood to mean that the human being gives up faith in his or her own intellectual adequacy to define the direction of Torah. It is not defeat in the sense that the student in the *beit midrash* would now say, "Yes, God, we will now follow revelation in order to define Halakhah," and "Torah is in heaven." On the contrary, R. Soloveitchik uses the midrashic stories in which God admits defeat in the *beit midrash* as a symbol of the divine intimacy with man.

> The strange Aggadic stories about a theoretical Halakhic "controversy" between the Almighty and Heavenly Academy and about R. Joshua b. Chanania's rejecting a Divine decision which favored a minority opinion over that of the majority are characteristic of the intimate Halakhic-covenantal relationship prevailing between man and God. Vide *Bava Mezi'a* 59b and 86a. (1965: 30 n)

The talmudic metaphor of the "defeat of God by his children," which celebrates the triumphant dignity of halakhic man's intellectual adequacy, is in no way negated in "The Lonely Man of Faith." On the contrary, it becomes a way of mediating how the relationship with God now bears the imprint of intensive intimacy. The notion of defeat in "The Lonely Man of Faith" is therefore not antithetical to the spirit of intellectual self-confidence and self-reliance that infuses the essay *Halakhic Man*. R. Soloveitchik can use the same rabbinic sources to serve the different purposes that different essays are meant to establish. In *Halakhic Man*, he is concerned with intellectual creativity, with halakhic man's uncompromising allegiance to truth, with the profound trust of halakhic man in rational argumentation. The master halakhist does not require illumination from a transcendental source in order to develop the Halakhah. In "The Lonely Man of Faith," by contrast, R. Soloveitchik is concerned with the way the Judaic tradition is fully awake to the way intimacy is expressed within the covenantal relationship with God. God's acceptance of the authority of the lower courts and God's smiling that "My children have defeated me" do not point in this essay to the celebration of intellectual creativity, but to the relational passion that exists between the man of faith and God.

"The Lonely Man of Faith" is not a halakhic anthropology; it does not attempt to present the worldview of a culture defined exclusively by mitzvot and traditional Torah learning. Rather, R. Soloveitchik is concerned to show that the relational passion found in Adam the second is also fully appreciated within the Jewish experience. Consequently, it is a mistake to pit the religious anthropology of "The Lonely Man of Faith" against that of *Halakhic Man* as if they were addressing the same issue in different ways.

THE UNIVERSALITY OF
COVENANTAL FAITH

What creates the impression that R. Soloveitchik is not addressing himself to a universal religious experience is his use of the term "covenant," which in the biblical tradition is used primarily in relation to Israel. The Sinai covenant is a specific moment in the history of this particular community; it is not a universal category. Thus, R. Soloveitchik's use of the term "covenantal faith community" seems to suggest that he is referring exclusively to the Jewish people. Upon careful reading of this essay, however, one sees that the term is not used only to describe the historical development in which Israel became an elect people, but in a much wider sense to denote a perspective through which any religious personality may perceive itself, the other, the world, and the meaning of the religious life.

> The community-fashioning gesture of Adam the first is, as I indicated before, purely utilitarian and intrinsically egotistic and, as such, rules out sacrificial action. For Adam the second, communicating and communing are redemptive sacrificial gestures. Thus, in crisis and distress there was planted the seed of a new type of community—the faith community which reached full fruition in the covenant between God and Abraham. (1965: 26)

The seeds of this new community have already been planted in Adam. The awareness of one's isolation from nature, the knowledge that there is nothing in the natural world that can provide human beings with the sense of identity and purpose, the sense that only through meeting another singular human being and forging a relationship of commitment and friendship with the other—all these find their full fruition in Abraham, but they do not belong exclusively to Abraham. The covenantal moment of Abraham can be understood only after being placed within the universal framework of Adam the second.

The creation story thus provides the subjective experiential foundations that infuse the covenantal faith consciousness. In neither the first nor the second chapters of Genesis does the Bible explicitly describe Adam as entering a covenant with God, nor is R. Soloveitchik referring here—as Kaplan supposes—to the covenant with Noah. It is clear that he is not concerned here with biblical history, but rather is using traditional language to describe a certain type of religious encounter. The first creation story provides the basis of a cosmic mode of understanding the religious life, the second that of an intimate communal way of living the religious life. The cosmic creates a community of interests; the covenantal, a community of commitments.

In the cosmic mode of self-understanding, the human being

does not understand or even know of the category of loneliness; it is simply not part of the frame of reference. Adam the first does not seek redemption. For R. Soloveitchik, this implies that he does not seek friendship or a community of commitments that requires sacrificial action, defeat, and forgoing success, all of which are essential components of the emergence of a community of shared purpose and total commitment.

The covenantal faith community of Adam the second, by contrast, has all those components. Moreover, when human beings meet each other to form this existential community, they discover a new way of encountering God.

> God is never outside of the covenantal community. He joins man and shares in his covenantal existence. Finitude and infinity, temporality and eternity, creature and creator become involved in the same community. They bind themselves together and participate in a unitive existence. (1965: 28)

The God encountered in this covenantal moment remains always present for covenantal man, unlike the God who appears through the medium of the cosmic drama. In the latter, there are moments of presence and hiddenness; there are times when everything in nature breathes the presence of God, but others when man senses God's total absence. In saying that "God is never outside of the covenantal community," accordingly, R. Soloveitchik means that the oscillation between divine presence and absence in the cosmic drama is not a part of the covenantal faith experience.

> The cosmic experience is antithetic and tantalizing. It exhausts itself in the awesome dichotomy of God's involvement in the drama of creation, and His exaltedness above and remoteness from this very drama. This

dichotomy cancels the intimacy and immediacy from one's relationship with God and renders the personal approach to God complicated and difficult. . . . Therefore, the man of faith, in order to redeem himself from his loneliness and misery, must meet God at a personal covenantal level, where he can be near Him and feel free in His presence. . . .

However, covenantal man of faith craving for a personal and intimate relation with God could not find it on the cosmic E-lohim encounter and had to shift his transcendental experience to a different level at which the finite "I" meets the infinite He "face to face." This strange communal relation between man and God is symbolized by the Tetragrammaton which therefore appears in the Biblical account of Adam the second. (1965: 31–33)

The covenantal faith experience is therefore free of the paradox of intimacy and absence, because God is never absent from the covenantal faith community. In this mode, it is possible for the identity of the human being to be whole. This applies to everything one builds in relationship with others, to one's ability to love and to move toward the other, to one's sense that the universe is a relational world and that it is only in the framework of the relational that one discovers the meaning of "to be." It is a reality constituted by presence of and relational intensity to the other and by the possibility of achieving this new form of wholeness through acts of commitment and love. In this world, therefore, God is known by the Tetragrammaton; God is addressed by a personal name. If God were not part of this community, then in-depth relational experience would be impossible from a religious perspective.

The change from a technical utilitarian relationship to a covenantal existential one occurs in the following manner. When God joins the community of man the miracle of revelation takes place in two dimensions: in the transcendental—*Deus absconditus* emerges suddenly as *Deus revelatus*—and in the human—homo absconditus sheds his mask and turns into homo revelatus. With the sound of the divine voice addressing man by his name, be it Abraham, Moses, or Samuel, God, whom man has searched along the endless trails of the universe, is discovered suddenly as being close to and intimate with man, standing just opposite or beside him. At this meeting—initiated by God—of God and man, the covenantal-prophetic community is established. When man addresses himself to God, calling Him in the informal, friendly tones of "Thou," the same miracle happens again: God joins man and at this meeting, initiated by man, a new covenantal community is born—the prayer community. (1965: 33–34)

R. Soloveitchik begins with the self-awareness of Adam the second, his experiential world with Eve, the process of self-discovery, the posing of questions of meaning, the perception of nature within qualitative terms, the mystery of immediacy—all of which flow from the subjective mode. As a religious personality, however, R. Soloveitchik has to shift away from the subjective framework to show that all this is possible only because of the way in which the reality of God is manifested to the human world. This decision of God creates a new experiential possibility and new normative aspirations.

Only when God emerged from the transcendent darkness of He-anonymity into the illumined spaces of
community-knowability and charged man with an
ethico-moral mission, did Adam *absconditus* and Eve *ab-*
scondita, while revealing themselves to God in prayer
and in unqualified commitment, also reveal themselves
to each other in sympathy and love on the one hand
and common action on the other. Thus, the final objective of the human quest for redemption was attained; the individual felt relieved from loneliness and
isolation. (1965: 45)

Through this process of mutual discovery, there is a con-
comitant shift in the character of the human community. Only now
has the possibility of friendship arisen—this too because of the new
revelatory reality of God.

The community of the committed became, ipso facto,
a community of friends—not of neighbors or acquain-
tances. Friendship—not as a social surface-relation
but as an existential in-depth relation between two
individuals—is realizable only within the framework of
the covenantal community where in-depth personalities relate themselves to each other ontologically and
total commitment to God and fellow-man is the order
of the day. In the majestic community, in which sur-
face-personalities meet and commitment never ex-
ceeded the bounds of the utilitarian, we may find
collegiality, neighborliness, civility, or courtesy—but
not friendship, which is the exclusive experience
awarded by God to covenantal man who is thus redeemed from his agonizing solitude. (1965: 45)

It would be absurd to imagine that R. Soloveitchik is here referring only to the Jewish community in using the term "covenantal," as if total commitment or authentic friendship were only possible within a halakhic community. The redemptive framework of mutual commitments, the ability to love, to enter into communal experiences going beyond utilitarian purposes, would certainly not be limited by him to Israel as a covenantal halakhic community. Covenant is a relational framework, descriptive of the quest for intimacy, in-depth relationship, sacrificial action, and the longing for a personal relationship with God. It is a perennial feature of the religious situation as perceived by Adam the second, which grows out of his human situation.

That the halakhic community of Judaism is simply a particular case of that universal human religious situation is indeed stated by Soloveitchik explicitly, while discussing the centrality of the norm in the divine-human encounter.

> Any encounter with God, if it is to redeem man, must be crystallized and objectified in a normative ethico-moral message. . . . The prophetic pilgrimage to God pursues a practical goal in whose realization the whole covenantal community shares. When confronted with God, the prophet receives an ethico-moral message to be handed down to and realized by the members of the covenantal community which is mainly a community in action. . . .
>
> The above-said, which is true of the universal faith community in general, has particular validity for the Halakhic community. The prime purpose of revelation in the opinion of the Halakhah is related to the giving of the Law. The God-man confrontation serves a didactic goal. (1965: 38–39, 40)

The centrality of the norm, from the perspective of the community of Adam the second, is thus present in "the universal faith community." Is this universal faith community a particular nation? Is it constituted by the covenant of Noah? R. Soloveitchik nowhere suggests this. Rather, it is rooted in the religious anthropology present in the creational framework. Creation provides two frameworks for perceiving the self and God, as well as for understanding interpersonal relationships and community. These two models can be seen not solely in the halakhic community but in all forms of human and religious culture.

R. Soloveitchik gives other clear hints of this. For instance, he writes in a footnote, "This paper refers to Adam the first as a type representing the collective human technological genius, and not to individual members of the human race" (1965: 14 n. **).

One can infer from this that Adam the second, too, refers to a universal human religious type that knows that there is no redemption without relational intensity. It is not solely the history of Judaism but the history of organized religion in general that shows that human beings can forfeit and misuse the covenantal faith moment in exploitative utilitarian, functional ways. Accordingly, R. Soloveitchik writes,

> The Biblical account of the original sin is the story of the man of faith who realizes suddenly that faith can be utilized for the acquisition of majesty and glory and who, instead of fostering a covenantal community, prefers to organize a political utilitarian community exploiting the sincerity and unqualified commitment of the crowd for non-covenantal, worldly purposes. The history of organized religion is replete with instances of desecration of the covenant. . . .

The prophet is a messenger carrying the great divine imperative addressed to a covenantal community. (1965: 27 n, 39)

Then after describing the centrality of the norm in prophecy, R. Soloveitchik adds,

The above-said, which is true of the universal faith community in general, has particular validity for the Halakhic community. The prime purpose of revelation in the opinion of the Halakhah is related to the giving of the Law. (1965: 40)

Clearly, for R. Soloveitchik, the norm is essential for both the halakhic and the universal faith communities. The description of the God-experience of Adam the second does not refer exclusively to those who live within the halakhic framework.

THE DIALECTICAL TENSION BETWEEN MAJESTY AND INTIMACY

R. Soloveitchik's typology and phenomenology of Adam the first and Adam the second are meant to illuminate the essential tension between living, on the one hand, in the framework of majesty, dignity, and control and, on the other, in the framework of relational passion, love, and sacrificial action. The oscillation between these two modes of making sense of God and reality is the permanent fate of the man of faith.

Dignity without relational intensity is a superficial way for an individual to organize his or her human reality; but neither is intimacy without dignity desirable. It is not, however, this dialectic as such that is responsible for the peculiar loneliness of the contemporary man of faith. Since the dialectical role has been assigned to humankind by God, it is God who wants the man of faith to oscillate between the faith community and the community of majesty, between being confronted by God in the cosmos and the intimate immediate apprehension of God through the covenant. It is rather the current widespread refusal to countenance this oscillation that gives rise to the special loneliness of men of faith today.

> While the ontological loneliness of the man of faith is due to a God-made and willed situation and is, as part of his destiny, a wholesome and integrating experience, the special kind of loneliness of contemporary men of faith referred to at the beginning of this paper is of a social nature due to a man-made historical situation and is, hence, an unwholesome and frustrating experience.
>
> Let me diagnose the situation in a few terse sentences. Contemporary Adam the first, extremely successful in his cosmic-majestic enterprise, refuses to pay earnest heed to the duality in man and tries to deny the undeniable, that another Adam exists beside or, rather, in him. By rejecting Adam the second, contemporary man, eo ipso, dismisses the covenantal faith community as something superfluous and obsolete. (1965: 55–56)

R. Soloveitchik hastens to add that he is not referring to militant atheism and the political community that propagates it. The problem lies rather with those who profess support of religion, yet increasingly evade the discomfort of its dialectic.

> I am referring rather to Western man who is affiliated with organized religion and is a generous supporter of

its institutions. He stands today in danger of losing his dialectical awareness and of abandoning completely the metaphysical polarity implanted in man as a member of both the majestic and covenantal community. Somehow, man of majesty considers the dialectical awareness too great a burden, interfering with his pursuit of happiness and success, and is, therefore, ready to cast it off. (1965: 56)

Here again, R. Soloveitchik states clearly that it is Western man, not just halakhic man, who stands in danger of losing his dialectical awareness. It is the same tendency discussed by R. Soloveitchik in his lengthy introductory footnote to *Halakhic Man* (pp. 139–43 n. 4), where he so strongly criticized those who seek in religion some sort of peace of mind, bringing a totally utilitarian quid pro quo approach to the relationship to God.

THE EXPERIENTIAL DIMENSIONS OF COVENANT AND REDEMPTION

Since "The Lonely Man of Faith," unlike *Halakhic Man*, is concerned with a universal condition of the faith experience, it is a mistake to see in the differences between the two essays a radical opposition that needs to be explained in the manner of Kaplan or of Singer and Sokol. On the contrary, in dealing with that universal condition and showing how it is exemplified in Judaism, the later essay draws upon the spirit of the earlier one and echoes many of its themes. The normative perspective that R. Soloveitchik brought to dogmatic notions such as providence, prophecy, and creation in *Halakhic Man* is continued in "The Lonely Man of Faith." The focus on experientializing metaphysical faith assertions is what enables R. Soloveitchik in "The Lonely Man of Faith" to give such a radically new appreciation of concepts such as covenant and redemption.

Not only is the notion of covenant experientialized, but also, as we have seen, the category of redemption is removed from its historical context of the national liberation of a particular community. Redemption becomes an existential category, directed toward the need for friendship and the overcoming of loneliness. Similarly, the discussion of prophecy in "The Lonely Man of Faith" has nothing to do with the metaphysical condition needed in order to make sense of prophecy or with the contents and circumstances of revelation, but with the existential need for intimacy with a personal God. In *Halakhic Man*, the prophet and not revelation was discussed; this served R. Soloveitchik's particular purpose there because it suggested the way the Jewish tradition celebrates uniqueness and self-creation. In *Halakhic Man*, the prophet is the symbol of the single one who breaks with social conformity. In "The Lonely Man of Faith," however, it is not the single one that is the issue, but the way that different manifestations of God make possible new modes of in-depth personal relationships. The yearning for covenantal intimacy can be initiated either by God through revelation or through the community by prayer.

> Prayer and prophecy are two synonymous designations of the covenantal God–man colloquy. Indeed, the prayer community was born the very instant the prophetic community expired and, when it did come into the spiritual world of the Jew of old, it did not supersede the prophetic community but rather perpetuated it. Prayer is the continuation of prophecy and the fellowship of prayerful men is ipso facto the fellowship of prophets. The difference between prayer and prophecy is, as I have already mentioned, related not to the substance of the dialogue but rather to the order in

which it is conducted. While within the prophetic community God takes the initiative—He speaks and man listens—in the prayer community the initiative belongs to man: he does the speaking and God, the listening. The word of prophecy is God's and is accepted by man. The word of prayer is man's and God accepts it. (1965: 35–36)

Since intimacy with God is essential to the life of the Judaic community, when God ceased to speak through the mouths of the biblical prophets, Jews decided that they would continue to speak to God. Thus the Judaic covenantal community turned from a prophetic community into a prayer community. From R. Soloveitchik's viewpoint, there is no fundamental difference between the two communities; they flow into each other.

This is a surprising position to be adopted by an Orthodox halakhist, whose entire religious system is built upon the premise of the literal truth of the word of revelation and the absolute authority of Torah and Halakhah. Our surprise diminishes, however, when we realize that this premise was indeed relevant to the concern of *Halakhic Man,* but not to that of "The Lonely Man of Faith." The latter is not an essay written to expound and defend the foundations of Jewish faith and Jewish halakhic commitment, but one that uses the Jewish tradition to illuminate a universal condition. Accordingly, the emphasis is not on the content of revelation but on the experiential necessity for revelation. This experiential necessity can be satisfied not only through the mode of revelation but also through the mode of prayer. In revelation, it is God who initiates the relational intimacy and the human being who responds to God's call. In prayer, it is the human being who initiates the longing for intimacy and God who is present.

R. Soloveitchik is not dealing here with the halakhic requirements of prayer or with the language of prayer, just as earlier in the essay he was not dealing with the language of revelation. He is quick to point out that prayer consists fundamentally in finding oneself in the presence of God.

> Prayer is basically an awareness of man finding himself in the presence of and addressing himself to his Maker, and to pray has one connotation only; to stand before God. To be sure, this awareness has been objectified and crystallized in standardized, definitive texts whose recitation is obligatory. The total faith commitment tends always to transcend the frontiers of fleeting, amorphous subjectivity and to venture into the outside world of the well-formed, objective gesture. However, no matter how important this tendency on the part of the faith commitment is—and it is of enormous significance in Halakhah which constantly demands from man that he translate his inner life into external facticity—it remains unalterably true that the very essence of prayer is the covenantal experience of being together with and talking to God and that the concrete performance such as the recitation of texts represents the technique of implementation of prayer and not prayer itself. In short prayer and prophecy are two synonymous designations of the covenantal God-man colloquy. (1965: 35–36)

Petitional prayer, which is so central in the Jewish liturgy, is merely the technical form of implementing that primary and universal divine-human encounter that precedes the specific content that the Jewish tradition brought into it. Fundamentally, prayer surfaces as a central category due to the need for an intimate relationship with God. When, in the time of Ezra, prophecy ceased being the mode through which Jews gave expression to this longing for intimacy, the men of the Great Assembly initiated a new way of continuing the prophetic faith covenantal community by becoming the prayer community.

Like the prophetic community that was its antecedent, the prayer community is one of empathy, concern, and love. Covenantal man does not only pray for himself; he is not trapped in his own ego, because what fundamentally characterizes his commitment to the other is self-transcendence, the movement of concern and responsibility. Therefore, R. Soloveitchik says, the Jewish community understood this as an essential feature of the character of the worshipful person. Accordingly, Judaism gave expression to this idea by requiring sacrificial moral action as an essential condition of the life of prayer. Prayer is not just seeking God through language and beseeching divine grace. The prayer community is a community of action, a community of the committed that is prepared to shoulder the burden of responsibility. Its acceptance of changed circumstances is not a passive resignation. It reflects an essential theme of Halakhah in which worship of God is not restricted to the synagogue but is expressed in the totality of moral concerns that one brings to living in society.

Authentic prayer can be performed only by a human being who has given up the impersonal universe, whose major concern is not mastery. Such prayer can emerge only in a community that has established the goals of redemption, friendship, and communal sharing as the essential salient features of what makes for a full human life.

Job, in R. Soloveitchik's interpretation, undergoes a radical transformation exemplified by the change in his approach to prayer. He begins by living a cosmic religious life in which his prayer is self-centered, made on behalf of his own family. The initial portrait of Job is one of Adam the first. It is when Job learns the art of empathy and the art of prayer, when he discovers concern for the other, that he becomes a covenantal man of faith.

Job failed to understand the covenantal nature of the prayer community in which destinies are dovetailed, suffering or joy is shared and prayers merge into one petition on behalf of all. As we all know, Job's sacrifices were not accepted, Job's prayers remained unheard, and Job—pragmatic Adam the first—met with catastrophe and the whirlwind uprooted him and his household. Only then did he discover the great covenantal experience of being together, praying together and for one another. "And the Lord turned the captivity of Job, when he prayed for his friends; also the Lord gave Job twice as much as he had before." Not only was Job rewarded with a double measure in material goods, but he also attained a new dimension of existence—the covenantal one. (1965: 38)

Note that for many rabbinic authorities, Job is not part of the halakhic tradition. The Book of Job does not tell us of any covenant of God with Job. If we understand covenant, however, not as a historical revelatory moment with a specific historical content but as an experiential way of organizing one's own religious life, then it becomes intelligible how R. Soloveitchik sees Job shift from being a person ignorant of the art of prayer to being one who, in discovering the other, has also discovered a new covenantal relationship with God.

In "The Lonely Man of Faith," R. Soloveitchik's comparative lack of interest in the events of history, and his placing greater emphasis on the experiential appropriation of religious language and dogmas, is understandable if we recognize the centrality of practice in his Judaic anthropology. A tradition that placed such emphasis on what one does, and not only on what one understands, lends itself easily to the translation of metaphysical claims into normative experiential ones. This was the way in which

Halakhic Man approached the theological claims of providence, creation, prophecy, and *teshuvah*.

This indifference to history, characteristic of a certain way of looking at the halakhic experience, enables us to understand how, for R. Soloveitchik, God is never absent from Judaic religious life. Prophecy moves into prayer; God can be addressed as "Thou." The Halakhah commands Jews to pray every day. Just as in *Halakhic Man* the mitzvah validates human dignity, because God could not issue commands if there were no faith in the human ability to implement those commands, there cannot be a mitzvah of prayer unless God is always present in a personal mode, capable of being addressed in the intimate language of the second person.

How does R. Soloveitchik know that God is responsive to this human call to God? Is it not possible to claim that the absence of prophecy signals that God has abandoned the community, that God is no longer available in any relational sense? Not so, in R. Soloveitchik's portrait of covenantal man. Rather, it is the step whereby God now energizes the covenantal partner to believe in the latter's own ability to initiate relational intimacy. The absence of prophecy does not signal rejection of covenantal man on the part of God, but rather, the call for him to become the active partner in the relationship.

The movement from prophecy to prayer parallels the movement from the prophet to the rabbinic sage of the *beit midrash*. God no longer pronounces on the development of the Halakhah. God wants the human partner alone to take responsibility for its content. Similarly, God does not initiate the intensity of relationship, but seeks that it be initiated by the covenantal partner. In that sense, there is a deep parallelism between the way in which prayer replaces prophecy and the way that the Torah scholar in the development of the oral tradition follows the mode of the prophet and revelation in formulating Torah and mitzvot.

During prayer and during Torah learning, the halakhist met

God in the intensity of relationship. In other moments, the halakhist continues the spirit of that intimacy by living a total life engaged by the daily concerns of humanity, fully aware that the mode of intimacy that comes through learning and prayer is not being violated or rejected, but rather, being translated into a new mode of being—namely, to live as a covenantal faith person in the majestic world. Consequently, the activist thrust does not have the enormous relational intensity, awareness, and intimacy that prayer and learning create. But this alternation is willed by a religious worldview that seeks both intimacy and creative activism in shaping and transforming the world.

As a halakhist, R. Soloveitchik has little in common with the event-based theology of Martin Buber and others, in which historical events mediate God's presence or absence. Instead, he has a tradition in which one feels the presence of God through Torah, prayer, and mitzvot. As long as a Jew can study Torah and the mitzvah is binding, God is present. Likewise, the world of the personal, of total normative commitment, of sacrificial love, could not surface as a human possibility were prayer not a permanent possibility in human experience.

This is a strange theological argument. It would appear that the man of faith decides upon God's presence or absence. Where is God's freedom? How do we not await God's confirmation regarding our deepest religious needs?

One could present a significant argument for the need for grace, for reading the signs of the calling, of deciphering God's decision regarding our relational needs. This is not the mode, however, that R. Soloveitchik the halakhist adopts in describing the universal faith condition. If Judaism is an illustration of how the lonely man of faith can understand himself, then he is given a tradition that has neutralized the need for God's direct miraculous involvement in order to understand what it is that God requires of humanity. A tradition that validates learning as a new path for developing the ongoing revelatory presence of God through Torah is a tradition that not only controls the content of God's word, but equally posits a notion of divine presence that flows from the certainty of a covenantal normative life rather than from external validation through miracle.

It is also in this regard that "The Lonely Man of Faith" builds upon many features of the Judaic outlook developed in *Halakhic Man:* the sense of human adequacy; the centrality of action; the normative experientializing of dogmatic claims; the indifference to miraculous revelations in history; the assurance that Torah study suffices to mediate and mirror God's eternal will. The covenantal Jewish experience likewise offers the universal faith community a God who is fully present to human beings if they seek not just to gain functional control but to understand the unique features of a covenantal faith experience that liberates Adam the second from his aloneness and offers him a world filled with possibilities of empathy, love, and sacrificial action. This human possibility will always be available to a religious person who knows that what God initiates and what a human being responds to are fundamentally integrated into a unified worldview.

Just as there is no separation between the written and the oral traditions, so is there no separation between the prophetic revelatory moment and the prayer moment. There is no effective difference between a biblical outlook, which reveals God's presence through miracles and redemptive dramatic moments, and a prayer-oriented outlook, which enables the categories of creation, revelation, redemption, and covenant to become the permanent legacy of all those who seek a covenantal faith experience.

5

CONFRONTATION

A THEOLOGICAL RESPONSUM

If my analysis of "The Lonely Man of Faith" is correct, how are we to understand R. Soloveitchik's theological responsum in "Confrontation," which limits Jewish-Christian discussion to what he calls the world of the secular, but keeps the faith experience of Judaism and of Christianity in total isolation from each other? If my reading of "The Lonely Man of Faith," which suggests that R. Soloveitchik believes there is a universal faith condition, of which Judaism is a profound illustration but not its exclusive expression, is correct, how can we explain R. Soloveitchik's claim in "Confrontation" that faith communities necessarily cannot share faith experiences with one another?

As the leading theologian and jurist of modern Orthodox Jewry, R. Soloveitchik was consulted on the question of Jewish-Christian dialogue in the 1960s, when Pope John XXIII opened up the Roman Catholic church in a quite unexpected way. Dialogue between Roman Catholics and others had suddenly become the order of the day. For instance, the Harvard Divinity School invited Catholics and Protestants to talk to each other at a major conference. Numerous invitations were issued by Catholic bodies to rabbis, who were pleased that important church figures finally wanted to engage them in serious theological discussions. At this time, Abraham Joshua Heschel was working very hard to get changes in the Roman Catholic liturgy. In brief, the Jewish world suddenly discovered that a major sector of the Christian world was inviting them to participate in the reformulation of its theological stance towards Judaism.

In "Confrontation," R. Soloveitchik sought to define the parameters that should guide the Orthodox rabbinate's response to the Second Vatican Council (1962–65), which signaled the Roman Catholic church's new openness to the Jewish people. Is dialogue between Christianity and Judaism possible? What issues should surface in the discussion after so many centuries of misunderstanding and of the preaching of contempt? Can triumphalist monotheistic faiths, after nurturing such distrust and delegitimization of alternative monotheistic traditions, suddenly engage themselves in serious theological reflection despite the history of religious prejudice and suspicion? Should there be a mutual examination of liturgy and theology? What should the Jew talk about today when invited by Christians to engage in religious discussion?

"Confrontation" addressed these questions as a rare theological responsum carrying the weight of a halakhic decision. None of R. Soloveitchik's other theological writings were understood to have the authority of Halakhah. In "The Lonely Man of Faith," for example, he stated explicitly that these writings are personal confessions of faith, laying no claim to halakhic authority (1965: 10). They are the attempt of an individual to unburden himself, to share his own inner religious life. "Confrontation," however, was treated as an authoritative response to a specific religious issue. Its closing paragraph includes the statement adopted by the Rabbinical Council of America, accepting R. Soloveitchik's theological position and obligating the Orthodox community to follow the guidelines laid down in the essay. If we measure a Jewish philosopher of the Orthodox tradition not only by his theological and psychological categories, not only by his aggadic midrashic thinking, but above all by his halakhic decisions regarding practice, then "Confrontation" is uniquely significant for evaluating R. Soloveitchik's thought.

R. Soloveitchik allows in "Confrontation" that Jews and Christians can meet to discuss the social and ethical problems they share. Simultaneously, however, he made a statement that was widely understood—rightly or wrongly—to forbid the discussion of theological matters in such meetings.

> The *logos*, the word, in which the multifarious religious experience is expressed, does not lend itself to standardization or universalization. The word of faith reflects the intimate, the private, the paradoxically inexpressible cravings of the individual for and his linking up with his Maker. It reflects the numinous character and the strangeness of the act of faith of a particular community which is totally incomprehensible to the man of a different faith community. Hence, it is important that the religious or theological *logos* should not be employed as the medium of communication between two faith communities whose modes of expression are as unique as their apocalyptic experiences. The confrontation should occur not at a theological, but at a mundane human level. There, all of us speak the universal language of modern man. As a matter of fact, our common interests lie not in the realm of faith, but in that of the secular orders. There we all face a powerful antagonist, we all have to contend with a considerable

number of matters of great concern. The relationship between two communities must be outer-directed and related to the secular orders with which men of faith come face to face. In the secular sphere we may discuss positions to be taken, ideas to be evolved, and plans to be formulated. In these matters, religious communities may together recommend action to be developed and may seize the initiative to be implemented later by general society. However, our joint engagement in this kind of enterprise must not dull our sense of identity as a faith community. We must always remember that our singular commitment to God and our hope and indomitable will for survival are non-negotiable and non-rationalizable and are not subject to debate and argumentation. The great encounter between God and man is a wholly personal private affair incomprehensible to the outsider—even to a brother of the same faith community. (1964: 23–24)

R. Soloveitchik is arguing that the faith moment is particularistic. And there is even a sense here that the individual's faith moment is not open to members of the same community. Now, although there are other such suggestions in R. Soloveitchik's writings, only very rarely is this radical thesis of the ultimate isolation of the faith experience expressed.

R. Soloveitchik's position in "Confrontation" seems quite strange in light of what he himself wrote in *Halakhic Man*, where his own religious phenomenology is deeply influenced by Kierkegaard, Barth, and Otto—individuals who come out of the Protestant Christian tradition. That whole essay, as we saw, brings the Jewish experience of Halakhah into discussion with theologians and philosophers who are in no way part of the Jewish tradition. There, to present the depth of the antinomies and contradictions

present in his understanding of the faith experience, R. Soloveitchik avails himself of categories taken from Otto, Kierkegaard, and
Barth.

> Even though Kierkegaard disagreed with Hegel's phi-
> losophy . . . , he, nevertheless, accepted from him the
> dialectical principle (with many significant changes, to
> be sure). And this concept of the dialectic, which he
> and Karl Barth introduced into the analysis of the un-
> folding of the religious consciousness, and this view
> concerning the antinomic structure of religious expe-
> rience, which was revised and refined by Rudolf Otto
> in his book, *The Idea of the Holy,* give the lie to the posi-
> tion that is prevalent nowadays in religious circles,
> whether in Protestant groups or in American Reform
> and Conservative Judaism, that the religious experi-
> ence is of a very simple nature—that is, devoid of the
> spiritual tortuousness present in the secular cultural
> consciousness of psychic upheavals, and of the pangs
> and torments that are inextricably connected with the
> development and refinement of man's spiritual per-
> sonality. (1983: 139–40 n. 4)

In *Halakhic Man,* R. Soloveitchik constantly moves back
and forth between Jewish and Christian sources. For example, Max
Scheller is important for R. Soloveitchik's understanding of repentance. Moreover, consider the whole list of non-Jewish writers
whom he quotes to emphasize the central role that self-creation
plays in Judaism.

> An echo of the longing for creativity, the ultimate
> desire of Judaism, makes itself heard in the philosophy
> of Kant, which is based upon the principle of the

spontaneity of the spirit in general, and in the neo-
Kantian school of Hermann Cohen, in the concept of
the creative pure thought in particular.

This concept of the obligatory nature of the creative
gesture, of self-creation as an ethical norm, an exalted
value, which Judaism introduced into the world, rever-
berates with particular strength in the worldviews of
Kierkegaard, Ibsen, Scheler, and Heidegger. (1983:
163–64 n. 147)

It is therefore clear that Christian writings illuminate and make intelligible what the Jewish faith experience is about. If the faith experience were so particular and sui generis, it would be impossible
for these Christian writers, whose language is totally other than halakhic discourse, to illuminate and make one understand the Jewish faith gesture.

What happened in the interim that led R. Soloveitchik to
make the astonishing claim in "Confrontation" that the faith experience cannot be intelligible to people outside of one's own faith?
Singer and Sokol find this statement in "Confrontation" so unintelligible that they can explain it only by some deep psychological
problem that R. Soloveitchik has with modernism, by "a lingering
concern over what they would say in 'Brisk' [the talmudic tradition
of R. Soloveitchik's family]."

Is it going too far to maintain that Soloveitchik's
strangely negative attitude toward inter-religious dialogue is prompted by a lingering concern over what they
would say in "Brisk." Of course, there is nothing strange
per se in the view that Jews should desist from discussing matters of faith with Christians or others. This position may easily be sustained on both prudential and

theological grounds. Soloveitchik himself has chosen the latter route, arguing in "Confrontation" "the word of faith reflects the intimate, the private, the paradoxically inexpressible cravings of the individual for . . . his Maker. It reflects the numinous character and the strangeness of the act of faith of a particular community which is totally incomprehensible to the man of a different faith community." Fair enough, but how can Joseph Soloveitchik say this? Has he not read widely in Christian theology? Does he not point to Kierkegaard, Barth, and Otto as thinkers who have plumbed the depths of religious experience? Most importantly, has he not drawn on these Christian theologians in formulating his own Jewish theology? If, despite all this, Soloveitchik can take a stand in opposition to interfaith discussions, it seems likely that, deep down, he feels a certain amount of guilt over what he is doing. After all, in "Brisk" the talmudists did not read Christian religious works. That much restraint—and here Soloveitchik's modernity again comes to the fore—he is not prepared to show. But at least, Soloveitchik apparently feels that there is no need to talk to the *goyim* in public.[9]

I believe that "Confrontation" is not R. Soloveitchik's attempt to keep the Jewish tradition, the world of Brisk, insulated from the dangerous influences of Western thought. The essay cannot simply be reduced to R. Soloveitchik's alleged personal psychological conflicts with his past. This type of reductionism avoids a serious analysis of the important arguments he presents in "Confrontation."

---

[9]Singer and Sokol, "Joseph Soloveitchik," 255.

The standard approach to what R. Soloveitchik writes in "Confrontation" does not do justice to the complexity of his arguments. If R. Soloveitchik's thesis were that the faith experience is radically private, he would not bother with the second part of this essay, where he does allow for certain kinds of interchanges between Judaism and Christianity. And if he did not include the second part of the essay, one could argue that his statements about the private nature of faith would equally prohibit intra-Jewish dialogue. R. Soloveitchik would then seem to have to accept a position that would rule out the possibility of Jews communicating their faith experiences even to other Jews. But this would have been a strange argument for a rabbi who taught Torah and spoke so passionately about *teshuvah* and prayer. R. Soloveitchik was a very communicative teacher. Therefore, the intensely private and incommunicable nature of the faith experience cannot be his final word on Jewish-Christian dialogue.

The article "Confrontation" requires a multileveled analysis that appreciates a variety of psychological, philosophical, and historical factors. If we look closely at the arguments presented in the essay, we find that R. Soloveitchik is not proscribing Jewish-Christian dialogue but setting limits and outlining a way for the dialogue to occur on both social matters and matters of faith that does not contradict his other writings but, in fact, is consistent with them.

THE PHILOSOPHICAL ANTHROPOLOGY OF "CONFRONTATION"

As in a number of his other essays, R. Soloveitchik's philosophical anthropology emerges in "Confrontation" through his midrashic reading of the creation story in Genesis. The difference between "The Lonely Man of Faith" and "Confrontation" can be clearly seen in R. Soloveitchik's differing interpretations of the existential condition reflected in the biblical account of Adam and Eve. In "The Lonely Man of Faith," R. Soloveitchik is concerned with the issue of human loneliness and how it may be overcome or how human beings can find "redemption."

> If Adam is to bring his quest for redemption to full re-alization, he must initiate action leading to the discov-ery of a companion who, even though as unique and singular as he, will master the art of communicating and, with him, form a community. . . .
>
> Therefore . . . Adam the second must quest for a dif-ferent kind of community. . . . His quest is for a new kind of fellowship which one finds in the existential community. (1965: 27–28)

There, R. Soloveitchik argues that human love is possible and that Adam the second overcomes the tragic sense of human loneliness. In "Confrontation," on the other hand, he emphasizes the radical isolation of the human being and states that, fundamentally, no love, no human relationship, can ever free one from the burden of his or her own tragic singularity and uniqueness.

> In all personal unions such as marriage, friendship, or comradeship, however strong the bonds uniting two individuals, the *modi existentiae* remain totally unique and hence, incongruous, at both levels, the ontological and the experiential. . . . In fact, the closer two individuals get to know each other, the more aware they become of the metaphysical distance separating them. Each one exists in a singular manner, completely absorbed in his individual awareness which is egocentric and exclu-sive. . . . It is paradoxical yet nonetheless true that each

human being lives both in an existential community, surrounded by friends, and in a state of existential loneliness and tension, confronted by strangers. In each to whom I relate as a human being, I find a friend, for we have many things in common, as well as a stranger, for each of us is unique and wholly other. This otherness stands in the way of complete mutual understanding. The gap of uniqueness is too wide to be bridged. Indeed, it is not a gap, it is an abyss. (1964: 15–16)

These interpretations would seem to indicate that he uses the Adam and Eve story differently depending upon the particular position for which he is arguing. In "The Lonely Man of Faith," he wants to build the anthropological foundations for an existential covenantal community. In his argument limiting Jewish-Christian dialogue in "Confrontation," he wants to argue for learning to live alone, to live with separateness. Therefore, his anthropological paradigm in "Confrontation" has a heuristic value, but does not necessarily reflect his total conception of the human condition and of the faith commitment.

THREE HUMAN MODELS

Non-confrontation

In "Confrontation," R. Soloveitchik discusses three images of the human condition. The first is natural man, who lives in total harmony with nature and exhibits no separate selfhood. The "I" is absorbed by the womb of nature and lives with nature's rhythms. This portrait is similar to Kierkegaard's aesthetic or hedonistic stage, in which human existence is not regarded as at all problematic. R.

Soloveitchik argues that there are modern representatives of this type of person and gives them the label "non-confronted man."

> Man who was created out of the dust of the ground, enveloped in a mist rising from the jungle, determined by biological immediacy and mechanical necessity, knows of no responsibility, no opposition, no fear, and no dichotomy, and hence he is free from carrying the load of humanity.
>
> In a word, this man is a non-confronted being. He is neither conscious of his assignment vis-à-vis something which is outside of himself nor is he aware of his existential otherness as a being summoned by his Maker to rise to tragic greatness.
>
> When I refer to man at the level of naturalness, I have in mind not the *Urmensch* of bygone times but modern man. I am speaking not in anthropological but typological categories. For non-confronted man is to be found not only in the cave or the jungle but also in the seats of learning and the halls of philosophers and artists. Non-confrontation is not necessarily restricted to a primitive existence but applies to human existence at all times, no matter how cultured and sophisticated. The *hedone*-oriented, egocentric person, the beauty-worshipper, committed to the goods of sense and craving exclusively for boundless aesthetic experience, the voluptuary, inventing needs in order to give himself the opportunity of continual gratification, the sybarite, constantly discovering new areas where pleasure is pursued and happiness found and lost, leads a non-confronted existence. (1964: 6–7)

Single-Confrontation

In the second model, separateness and self-consciousness are experienced. We could call it the subject-object relationship to nature, in which man becomes aware that he is not one with nature; he is a subject and the natural world is an object. It is at this point that the cognitive and normative gestures begin for R. Soloveitchik. The cognitive gesture involves attempts to master nature and the normative gesture involves not mastery, but what he calls "defeat" or "surrender."

> As we stated previously, non-confronted man is a non-normative being. The second story is of confronted man who began to appraise critically his position vis-à-vis his environment and found his existential experience too complex to be equated with the simplicity and non-directedness of the natural life-stream. This man, as a subject-knower facing an almost impenetrable objective order, was dislocated by God from his position of naturalness and harmonious being and placed in a new existential realm, that of confronted existence. Confronted man is a displaced person. . . . At this phase, man, estranged from nature, fully aware of his grand and tragic destiny, became the recipient of the first norm—"And the Lord God commanded the man" (Gen. 2:16). The divine imperative burst forth out of infinity and overpowered finite man. . . .
>
> The reason for the failure of confronted man to play his role fully lies in the fact that, while the cognitive gesture gives man mastery and a sense of success, the normative gesture requires of man surrender. At this juncture, man of today commits the error which his ancestor, Adam of old, committed by lending an

142

attentive ear to the demonic whisper "Ye shall be as God, knowing good and evil." (1964: 13)

In the normative or ethical gesture, one is not in control. On the contrary, one is called upon to surrender to the demands of the norm, one is mastered—and thus "defeated"—by the moral norm. This second anthropological model, then, is of the conscious person, who is aware that there is a struggle with nature and is called upon to build human communities, to overcome disease, and to build a social human world guided by principles of justice.

Double-Confrontation

The third anthropological model involves man's confrontation not with nature but with the interpersonal relationship symbolized by the encounter between Adam and Eve in the second creation story. R. Soloveitchik uses this model in explaining the problematic nature of Jewish-Christian dialogue.

> There is, however, a third level which man, if he is longing for self-fulfillment, must ascend. At this level, man finds himself confronted again. Only this time it is not the confrontation of a subject who gazes, with a sense of superiority, at the object beneath him, but of two equal subjects, both lonely in their otherness and uniqueness, both opposed and rejected by an objective order, both craving for companionship. . . .
> "And the Lord God said, It is not good that the man should be alone. I will make a helpmeet opposite him. . . . And the Lord God made the rib which he had taken from the man into a woman and brought her unto man." (Gen. 2:18, 22) God created Eve, another human being. Two individuals, lonely and helpless in

their solitude, meet, and the first community is formed. (1964: 14)

These are the same themes of loneliness, isolation, and uniqueness that, as we saw in the "The Lonely Man of Faith," are central to R. Soloveitchik's understanding of human relationships. There, he wrote,

> Adam the second is still lonely. He separated himself from his environment which became the object of his intellectual gaze. "And the man gave names to all the beasts and to the fowl of the heaven and to every animal of the field." He is a citizen of a new world, the world of man, but he has no companion with whom to communicate and therefore he is existentially insecure. Neither would the availability of the female, who was created with Adam the first, have changed this human situation if not for the emergence of a new kind of companionship. At this crucial point, if Adam is to bring his quest for redemption to full realization, he must initiate action leading to the discovery of a companion who, even though as unique and singular as he, will master the art of communicating and, with him, form a community. . . .
>
> For Adam the second, communicating and communing are redemptive sacrificial gestures. Thus, in crisis and distress there was planted the seed of a new type of community—the faith community which reached full fruition in the covenant between God and Abraham. (1965: 26–27)

In "Confrontation," however, R. Soloveitchik emphasizes instead the radical loneliness of the human being and states that, fundamentally, no love, no human relationship, can ever free one from the burden of his or her own tragic singularity and uniqueness.

> Our feelings of sympathy and love for our confronter are rooted in the surface personality and they do not reach into the inner recesses of our depth personality which never leaves its ontological seclusion and never becomes involved in a communal existence. (1964: 16)

R. Soloveitchik goes on to claim that modern man does not know how to live with the burden of relationship and aloneness and that therefore relationships turn into a quest for mastery and control.

> Modern man, who did not meet to the fullest the challenge of confrontation on the second level, does not perform well at the level of personal confrontation either. He has forgotten how to master the difficult dialectical art of being one with and, at the same time, different from, his human confronter, of living in community and simultaneously in solitude. He has developed the habit of confronting his fellow man in a fashion similar to that which prevails at the level of subject-object relationship, seeking to dominate and subordinate him instead of communicating and communing with him. The wondrous personal confrontation of Adam and Eve is thus turned into an ugly attempt at depersonalization. (1964: 16)

Behind every human relationship lurks the danger of human domination and exploitation. This anthropological insight will later be used in R. Soloveitchik's analysis of the dangers implicit in Jewish-Christian dialogue.

It is with the anthropology of the double-confronted man that R. Soloveitchik develops his preliminary position on Jewish-Christian dialogue. It is quite interesting that the model of loneliness and solitude is built upon the most intimate of relationships, that between Adam and Eve. Adam and Eve represent the longing for a human relationship, but one that cannot and must not remove ontological solitude and uniqueness. To ignore human solitude, uniqueness, and singularity is tantamount to destroying human dignity—the image of God in the human person.

What were the essential factors governing R. Soloveitchik's hesitancy or uneasiness regarding Jewish-Christian dialogue? After developing his model of confronted/non-confronted man, he shifts the discussion to an analysis of the double burden that Jews must always carry.

> We Jews have been burdened with a twofold task; we have to cope with the problem of a double confrontation. We think of ourselves as human beings, sharing the destiny of Adam in his general encounter with nature, and as members of a covenantal community which has preserved its identity under most unfavorable conditions, confronted by another faith community. We believe we are the bearers of a double charismatic load, that of the dignity of man and that of the sanctity of the covenantal community. In this difficult role, we are summoned by God, who revealed himself at both the level of universal creation and that of the private covenant, to undertake a double mission—the universal human and the exclusive covenantal confrontation. (1964: 17)

There are many Jews who appreciate the confrontation with nature, "the cosmic confrontation," where human beings feel called upon to eradicate disease, to advance science, technology, medicine, to overcome passivity and resignation in the face of human suffering. There are, however, Jews who cannot bear the burden of that confrontation which demands distinctiveness, solitude, and separateness.

R. Soloveitchik distinguishes between the traditional Jew who understood the meaning of double-confrontation and the Westernized emancipated Jew who sees the double-confrontation as an impossible burden.

> The Jew of old was a doubly confronted being. The emancipated modern Jew, however, has been trying for a long time, to do away with this twofold responsibility which weighs heavily upon him. The Westernized Jew maintains that it is impossible to engage in both confrontations, the universal and the covenantal, which, in his opinion, are mutually exclusive. (1964: 17)

Those who are eager to participate in the Jewish-Christian dialogue often reveal features of the single-confronted person and do not understand sufficiently the meaning of a total faith commitment and the burden of double-confrontation.

> They completely fail to grasp the real nature and the full implications of a meaningful Jewish identity.
>
> This failure rests upon two misconceptions of the nature of the faith community. First, the single-confrontation philosophy continues to speak of Jewish identity without realizing that this term can only be understood under the aspect of singularity and otherness. There is no identity without uniqueness. As there

147

cannot be an equation between two individuals unless they are converted into abstractions, it is likewise absurd to speak of the commensurability of two faith communities which are individual entities. (1964: 18)

R. Soloveitchik was worried about those Jews who, he believed, were prepared to compromise the unique destiny of the Jewish people in order to integrate fully into Western Christian society. He understood the longing to give up one's own particular identity and was frightened of the desire of Jews to run away from their distinctiveness. He was concerned that some people would enter discussions with Christians on the superficial level and say things like, "Aren't we all the same? You have priests; we have rabbis. You have Easter; we have Passover. You have Christmas; we have Hanukkah. We share a common kinship in faith. There are no ultimate differences between Christianity and Judaism."

R. Soloveitchik is filled with the memory of medieval Jewish-Christian disputations and is haunted by the specter of Christian anti-Semitism. He is aware of the heroism of the Jewish people to withstand persecution in the face of attempts to weaken their loyalty to the covenant of Torah and mitzvah. Any suggestion that Jews would be prepared, for the sake of acceptance by the Christian world, to give up elements of their tradition is vile to R. Soloveitchik.

> We certainly have not been authorized by our history, sanctified by the martyrdom of millions, to even hint to another faith community that we are mentally ready to revise historical attitudes, to trade favors pertaining to fundamental matters of faith, and to reconcile "some" differences. Such a suggestion would be nothing but a betrayal of our great tradition and heritage

and would, furthermore, produce no practical benefits. . . . We cannot command the respect of our con-
fronters by displaying a servile attitude. (1964: 25)

For R. Soloveitchik, the energy and vitality that empowers a
faith commitment is the belief that one's particular religious tradition is the true and exclusive way for the fulfillment of religious life.
It is not "a" way but "the" way. His argument regarding the importance of uniqueness and singularity is expressed theologically in
the following manner:

> The axiological awareness of each faith community is
> an exclusive one, for it believes—and this belief is in-
> dispensable to the survival of the community—that its
> system of dogmas, doctrines and values is best fitted for
> the attainment of the ultimate good. . . . Each faith
> community is unyielding in its eschatological expecta-
> tions. It perceives the events at the end of time with ex-
> ultant certainty and expects man, by surrender of
> selfish pettiness and by consecration to the great des-
> tiny of life, to embrace the faith that this community
> has been preaching throughout the millennia. Stan-
> dardization of practices, equalization of dogmatic cer-
> titudes, and the waiving of eschatological claims spell
> the end of the vibrant and great faith experience of any
> religious community. It is as unique and enigmatic as
> the individual himself. (1964: 19)

Although R. Soloveitchik set a personal example of living
the tension between interacting with Kierkegaard and Otto and engaging with the best of Western intellectual culture while devoting
his life to the study of Torah, his example has not been the norm
for the adjustment of traditional Orthodox Jews to the Western

world. R. Soloveitchik and Maimonides are examples of the way in which intense particularity and appreciation for the universal can live in the soul of the same individual. Maimonides can embrace Al Farabi, Ibn Bajja, and appreciate the world of Aristotle, using the rich Greek Islamic tradition for an understanding of his own biblical and rabbinic traditions. R. Soloveitchik can use the categories of Nietzsche, Kierkegaard, and Kant to illuminate the halakhic experience of his father, while never for a moment departing from his passion for the four cubits of the Halakhah. But, unfortunately, this kind of model and orientation has not succeeded in capturing the masses of Jews. One finds either those with "thin" identities, in which the element of the ethical and universal are emphasized, or those with "thick" identities, in which the focus is on the particular rituals and symbols of Halakhah.

I would argue that R. Soloveitchik does not close the door to Jewish-Christian discussions, but places very careful barriers, building a "fence" around the Torah, reminding Jews that there is a dimension to their faith that permanently condemns them to separateness and isolation. R. Soloveitchik seems to be saying that, on the one hand, he would allow certain individuals to participate in this discussion so long as they are aware that full communication is not possible. For R. Soloveitchik, they cannot share all things together, because there is no identity without uniqueness, singularity, and separateness. Therefore, in the dialogue with Christianity, he could trust only those Jews who could bear the burden of solitude. He could trust only those who would not be frightened by the intimate, personal features of Judaism, by the awareness that there will always be distance between Christians and Jews and that each faith has its distinct historical and eschatological beliefs. Only one who is not frightened of distance can build toward real relationships, because one who cannot handle his or her own uniqueness is ultimately either absorbed by the other (i.e., made into an object) or makes the other into an object. In either case, you have the danger of one side dominating the other, which is the antithesis to authentic dialogue. Only those who can live with what R. Soloveitchik calls double-confrontation can enter into Jewish-Christian dialogue.

This is the argument that R. Soloveitchik presents to Jews. There is, also, however a series of arguments, conditions, and warnings that he addresses to the Christian community.

ADDRESSING THE CHRISTIANS:
RESERVATIONS AND CONDITIONS

If we look at the history of Jewish-Christian confrontations, we see a great deal of evidence that Christians did not know how to talk with Jews in true mutual respect. Historically, the Jewish-Christian discussion has always been cast in terms of the alleged love and grace of the New Testament versus the vengeance and stern justice of the Old Testament. Alternatively, the discussion has revolved around the question "What was Judaism lacking that Christianity came to provide?" The Christian mode of dialogue was often an opportunity to present Christianity as the "fulfillment" of the promises of the Hebrew Bible. In the medieval context, such discussions took the form of debates or polemics, because the question was one of establishing the exclusive truth of a particular faith tradition or which community was God's elect and the recipient of divine providence. And given their position as a weak, subject people, Jews could not emerge from these discussions victorious.

Thus, the crucial questions to be asked today before entering into such dialogue are these: What are the categories through which we are going to speak and the parameters of the discussion? Who will set the theological frame of reference? Are we going to meet in order to discover that not all the Jews are guilty of deicide or that the law does not necessarily create perverted human beings?

R. Soloveitchik could not tolerate attempts to interpret Judaism in the theological categories of Christianity. There is nothing intrinsic to Judaism that requires Christianity. Judaism is not an incomplete revelatory framework that requires the Christian experience for its own fulfillment in history. Judaism and Christianity are two distinct faith communities, each one with its own self-understanding and way of life. Each must be understood in its own radical individuality. Neither one can absorb the other. For R. Soloveitchik, this would violate the intrinsic dignity and identity of each faith community.

> When God created man and endowed him with individual dignity, He decreed that the ontological legitimacy and relevance of the individual human being is to be discovered not without but within the individual. He was created because God approved of him as an autonomous human being and not as an auxiliary being in the service of someone else. The ontological purposiveness of his existence is immanent in him. The same is true of a religious community, whose worth is not to be measured by external standards. (1964: 23)

Judaism must be appreciated from within itself. Judaism must be articulated in its own categories and not discussed in a theological language that reduces the particularity and dignity of Judaism into some generalized notion that could be absorbed by the Christian experience.

For R. Soloveitchik, the very meaning of the creation of a single human life argues against making the individual an instrument for community or a faith community like Judaism as an instrument to prepare the way for the fuller realization of God's plan through Christianity.

We are a totally independent faith community. We do not revolve as a satellite in any orbit. Nor are we related to any other faith community as "brethren" even though "separated." People confuse two concepts when they speak of a common tradition uniting two faith communities such as the Christian and the Judaic. This term may have relevance if one looks upon a faith community under an historico-cultural aspect and interprets its relationship to another faith community in sociological, human, categories describing the unfolding of the creative consciousness of man. . . . However, when we shift the focus from the dimension of culture to that of faith—where total unconditional commitment and involvement are necessary—the whole idea of a tradition of faiths and the continuum of revealed doctrines which are by their very nature incommensurate and related to different frames of reference is utterly absurd, unless one is ready to acquiesce in the Christian theological claim that Christianity has superseded Judaism. (1964: 21–23)

In the wake of a very long Christian tradition of supersessionism vis-à-vis Judaism, R. Soloveitchik wants to make it as clear as possible that even the slightest hint of the presence of this ideology is absolutely unacceptable in Jewish-Christian dialogue. And a quick reading of this quotation might suggest that to avoid this possibility R. Soloveitchik is suggesting that no dialogue occur on matters of faith and theology. Yet, the proscription here is not against theological dialogue in toto but against the use of Christian "concepts" and "frames of reference" to discuss Judaism. R. Soloveitchik seeks to exclude the subtle and often unintended presence of supersessionism by delimiting the forms of language and discourse that are used in interfaith dialogue. A primary principle, therefore, is to stick to the particular language of your own faith. An interlocutor should never be "impelled to avail himself of the language of his opponent. This in itself would mean surrender of individuality and distinctiveness" (1964: 24).

GENUINE POSSIBILITIES FOR DIALOGUE

In R. Soloveitchik's theology, where the focus for understanding religious doctrines is experiential, there are rich new opportunities for genuine religious dialogue. For example, in *The Halakhic Mind*, R. Soloveitchik develops categories that he labels the "normative" and the "exoteric," which are shared by all faith communities. In the third chapter of *The Halakhic Mind* he argues strongly for the necessity of objectification and for the centrality of community and of the need for religious inwardness to be expressed in normative frameworks in order to retain its exoteric character. R. Soloveitchik's arguments against religious subjectivism are not related solely to Judaism, but are relevant to all theistic religions grounded in the belief in revelation. When he refers to Judaism in chapter four he writes,

> Objectification reaches its highest expression in the Halakhah. Halakhah is the act of seizing the subjective flow and converting it into enduring and tangible magnitudes. It is the crystallization of the fleeting individual experience into fixed principles and universal norms. In short, Halakhah is the objectifying instrument of our religious consciousness, the form-principle of the transcendental act, the matrix in which the amorphous religious hylo is cast. (1986: 85)

The centrality of Halakhah in Judaism is the highest expression of the need to objectify religious inwardness; it is not, however, the only expression of this vital religious process. Similarly, in "The Lonely Man of Faith" R. Soloveitchik writes of the tendency to "transcend the frontiers of fleeting, amorphous subjectivity and to overture into the outside world of the well-formed, objective gesture. However, no matter how important this tendency on the part of the faith commitment is—and it is of enormous significance in Halakhah, which constantly demands from man that he translate his inner life in external facticity . . . " (1965: 35).

In a medieval context, where the focus was on proving historical truth claims and on validating religious dogma, there was built-in hostility between different faith communities. In the modern world, however, when concerns have come to focus on the issue of how religious values are internalized and how they shape human character, new possibilities for dialogue between the faiths have opened up. In contrast to medieval Jewish philosophers, R. Soloveitchik reinterpreted the doctrines of prophecy and divine providence into experiential and normative categories. In *Halakhic Man*, as we saw, he wrote,

> Man is obliged to broaden the scope and strengthen the intensity of the individual providence that watches over him. Everything is dependent on him; it is all in his hands. When a person creates himself, ceases to be a mere species man, and becomes a man of God, then he has fulfilled that commandment which is implicit in the principle of providence. (1983: 128)

If divine providence is thus a normative demand to become a unique individual and to resist the faceless mediocrity of mass culture, then the central concern of religious life is no longer the metaphysical question of the medieval period, "Toward whom does God show individual providence?" but rather, "How do I become a self-creating person?" Jews and Christians can engage in a common theological discussion on how their respective traditions can develop self-creative personalities in opposition to the faceless homogenization of modern culture. The experiential dimension of faith, then, can provide the foundations for serious discussion and new learning possibilities between faith communities.

"CONFRONTATION" AS A POLITICAL RESPONSUM

R. Soloveitchik never repudiated intellectual study, mutual exchange of ideas, and the importance of making sense of Judaism within a larger intellectual frame of reference. I believe it is necessary that we make an important distinction that Singer and Sokol ignore. There is a difference between studying and being engaged as an individual with texts by Kierkegaard, Barth, Luther, or Augustine and being invited by others for a public confrontation that may lead to some form of accommodation and compromise. In other words, to R. Soloveitchik, the public dialogue is not a personal intellectual engagement with people of other faith commitments. It is more a public debate, usually designed to create reconciliation and accommodation. This has a totally different ambience than that suggested by intellectual study. When R. Soloveitchik is studying Kierkegaard, he is not dealing with the historical struggle of two faith communities. He is acting as an individual seeking to understand his own religious life. In "Confrontation" R. Soloveitchik is not returning out of guilt to the insulated intellectual ghetto of his grandfather's form of spirituality. Rather, "Confrontation" is a political responsum that addresses the issue of public and politically charged discussions between Judaism and Christianity as institutions. It is a response to the way Jews are to survive in an open society that offers both intellectual riches and the frightful reality of assimilation.

R. Soloveitchik did not reject the current openness of Christianity to Judaism, but was cautious and concerned with the way this discussion would be conducted. As a halakhic political leader of the Jews, who were then a community of the few and weak, still traumatized by the Holocaust, by the threat of assimilation, and by the loss of so many of their brothers and sisters within the communist orbit, he advises caution in public discussions with Christianity. At the same time, he wants to encourage Jews to discover a language of social concern and to show the West that there are no moral problems in the larger society to which Jews are indifferent.

That R. Soloveitchik saw "Confrontation" within a larger political context is clear from the end of his responsum, when he uses the midrashic model of Jacob confronting Esau to illuminate the confrontation between Christianity and Judaism. Esau was always the symbol of the larger powers of the West, hostile and frightening, that intimidated and sought Jewish destruction. The very name of the article, "Confrontation," indicates how this model shaped the context of R. Soloveitchik's public statement on Jewish-Christian dialogue in the twentieth century.

> Our representatives who meet with the spokesmen of the community of the many should be given instructions similar to those enunciated by our patriarch Jacob when he sent his agents to meet his brother Esau. (1964: 25–26)

Notice that R. Soloveitchik uses the words "our representatives." He is not speaking here of students who are studying together in university or theological colleges, or people wanting to study Talmud or New Testament thought or Thomas Aquinas or Maimonides together. Rather, it is an official political meeting of "representatives" and "spokesmen." R. Soloveitchik goes on to elaborate:

> What was the nature of these instructions? Our approach to and relationship with the outside world has always been of an ambivalent character, intrinsically antithetic, bordering at times on the paradoxical. We relate ourselves to and at the same time withdraw from, we come close to and simultaneously retreat from the world of Esau. When the process of coming nearer and nearer is almost consummated, we immediately begin to retreat quickly into seclusion. We cooperate with the members of other faith communities in all fields of constructive human endeavor, but, simultaneously with our integration into the general social framework, we engage in a movement of recoil and retrace our steps. In a word, we belong to the human society and, at the same time, we feel as strangers and outsiders. We are rooted in the here and now reality as inhabitants of our globe, and yet we experience a sense of homelessness and loneliness as if we belonged somewhere else. We are both realists and dreamers, prudent and practical on the one hand, and visionaries and idealists on the other. (1964: 26)

It is true that the halakhic decisions of a thinker such as R. Soloveitchik may be used as a gauge of his theological thought. However, "Confrontation," rather than repudiating the possibility of serious Jewish discussion with the West, welcomes it within the orbit of cultural experience, and even within the ambience of the faith experience, provided that each group frees itself of the theological categories that reduce the other to an instrument for its own success in history. Instrumentalizing the other, patronizing the other, seeing the other in terms of one's own political and spiritual aspirations do violence to the intrinsic dignity that the biblical concept of creation gives to "the other." To live with God the Creator is to live with the radical surprise and affirmation of "the other" in his or her full personhood and dignity and never to reduce any individual community into an object for suprapersonal, triumphalist self-aggrandizement.

Although R. Soloveitchik is committed to what I consider to be the problematic view that it is intrinsic to a faith community to believe in its vision as being best suited for the well-being of humanity and in the eventual universal acceptance of the truth of one's own faith commitment, nevertheless, within the present unredeemed world, R. Soloveitchik's relationship to other faiths is characterized by respect and acceptance.

And regardless of R. Soloveitchik's claim regarding each community's exclusive possession of truth, he provides a way of viewing the relationship between Judaism and Christianity within the model of the love relationship between Adam and Eve. This is a marriage relationship in which the separateness of each partner is a fundamental feature. Just as Christianity's perception of Judaism must be free from its own supersessionist claims, similarly, Judaism's perception of Christianity must be free of attempts to absorb it within the messianic historical destiny of Israel. The following statement in Maimonides' *Mishneh Torah* reflects how Christianity was interpreted in Jewish triumphalist eschatological categories.

> But it is beyond the human mind to fathom the designs of the Creator; for our ways are not His ways, neither are our thoughts His thoughts. All these matters relating to Jesus of Nazareth and the Ishmaelite (Mohammed) who came after him, only served to clear the way for King Messiah, to prepare the whole world to

worship God with one accord, as it is written, *For then will I turn to the peoples a pure language, that they may all call upon the name of the Lord to serve Him with one consent* (Zeph. 3:9). Thus the messianic hope, the Torah, and the commandments have become familiar topics—topics of conversation (among the inhabitants) of the far isles and many peoples, uncircumcised of heart and flesh. They are discussing these matters and the commandments of the Torah. Some say, "Those commandments were true, but have lost their validity and are no longer binding"; others declare that they had an esoteric meaning and were not intended to be taken literally; that the Messiah has already come and revealed their occult significance. But when the true King Messiah will appear and succeed, be exalted and lifted up, they will forthwith recant and realize that they have inherited naught but lies from their fathers, that their prophets and forbears led them astray. (*M.T. Book of Judges,* xxiii–xxiv)

THE COMPLEXITY OF LIVING ON TWO PLANES OF REALITY

I believe that R. Soloveitchik's position regarding Jewish-Christian dialogue appears to contradict his other theological essays only because of its complexity. He is both restricting and encouraging the dialogue because he sees many dangers and possible pitfalls in such an encounter. The greatest perplexity in the article stems, I believe, from R. Soloveitchik's assertion that Jews must live on two planes of reality. In the Rabbinic Council Record for 1966, R. Soloveitchik gave a clear and precise explanation of the directions for Jewish-Christian dialogue in the light of his idea of double-

confrontation. He begins by pointing explicitly to the two different ways Jews interact with others.

> On the one hand, Jews are vitally concerned with the
> problems affecting the common destiny of man. . . .
> On the other hand, we are a distinctive faith commu-
> nity with a unique commitment, singular relationship
> to God and a specific way of life. We must never con-
> fuse our role as the bearers of a particular commitment
> and destiny with our role as members of the family of
> man.
>
> In the area of faith, religious law, doctrine, and rit-
> ual, Jews have throughout the ages been a community
> guided exclusively by distinctive concerns, ideals, and
> commitments. Our love of and dedication to God are
> personal and bespeak an intimate relationship which
> must not be debated with others whose relationship to
> God has been molded by different historical events and
> in different terms. Discussion will in no way enhance
> or hallow these emotions. (Rabbinical Council Record
> for Feb. 1966, 78–80)

Having specified the two different modes, he then specifies
in detail how acceptable dialogue is in the first and how unacceptable in the second.

> We are, therefore, opposed to any public debate, dia-
> logue or symposium concerning the doctrinal, dog-
> matic, or ritual aspects of our faith vis à vis "similar"
> aspects of another faith community. We believe in and
> are committed to our Maker in a specific manner and
> we will not question, defend, offer apologies, analyze
> or rationalize our faith in dialogues centered about

these "private" topics which express our personal relationship to the God of Israel. . . . When, however, we
move from the private world of faith to the public
world of humanitarian and cultural endeavors, communication among the various faith communities
is desirable and even essential. . . . Jewish rabbis and
Christian clergymen cannot discuss socio-cultural and
moral problems as sociologists, historians or cultural
ethicists in agnostic or secularist categories. As men of
God, our thoughts, feelings, perceptions and terminology bear the imprint of a religious world outlook.

We define ideas in religious categories. In discussions we apply the religious yardstick and the religious
idiom. We evaluate man as the bearer of God's Like-
ness. We define morality as an act of *Imitatio Dei*, etc. In
a word, even our dialogue at a socio-humanitarian
level must inevitably be grounded in universal religious
categories and values. However, these categories and
values, even though religious in nature and biblical in
origin, represent the universal and public—not the individual and private—in religion. (Rabbinical Council
Record for Feb. 1966, 78–80)

The Jewish experience of faith is dual because God meets
humans on two planes of reality. Most of us find this perplexing because we recognize only a single confrontation. We are not prepared to live with particular identities and particularistic
requirements and at the same time see them in a universal historical framework. R. Soloveitchik is as critical of those who remain
only within the orbit of the halakhic world and believe there is no
cooperation possible between people of different religions as he is
of those who abandon their particularity for the sake of the universal. He asserts that intense revelatory faith commitments can be

seen simultaneously in generalized frames of reference that encourage religious commitment to the world.

There may be something healthy in stepping away from a frame of reference that separates and isolates the believer from the human "other" who is not connected to the same faith. And this is what the notion of double-confrontation allows for: to live both on the plane of the universal and on the plane of the particular as two distinct spiritual frames of reference. The implications of the double-confrontation for Jewish-Christian discussions are that they must take place on the level where a translation is possible and at the same time shy away from uncovering the intimate and the personal relationship of believers to God that is so crucial to the faith moment. What is very intimate and passionate and exclusive and has defined the very identity of a faith community is not something that you are required to make public and translate into a language that would weaken and neutralize the intimate framework of religious life.

R. Soloveitchik is aware that the faith experience is often interpreted in exclusivist language. Covenantal election and the Sinai experience are moments of intense intimacy. The language of intimacy conveys the sense of exclusivity. The following midrash expresses the intuitive sense of the particularity and exclusivity of divine love and election.

> R. Akiba says: I shall speak of the prophecies and the praises of Him by whose word the world came into being, before all the nations of the world. For all the nations of the world ask Israel, saying "What is thy beloved more than another beloved, that thou dost so adjure us" (Song of Songs 5:9), that you are so ready to die for Him, and so ready to let yourselves be killed for Him?—For it is said: "Therefore do the maidens love Thee" (ibid. 1:3), meaning, they love Thee unto death.

And it is also written: "Nay but for Thy sake are we killed all the day" (Ps. 44:23). "—You are handsome, you are mighty, come and intermingle with us." But the Israelites say to the nations of the world: "Do you know Him? Let us but tell you some of His praise: 'My beloved is white and ruddy,'" etc. (Song of Songs 5:10). As soon as the nations of the world hear some of His praise, they say to the Israelites: "We will join you," as it is said: "Whither is thy beloved gone, O thou fairest among women? Whither hath thy beloved turned him, that we may seek him with thee" (ibid. 6:1). The Israelites, however, say to the nations of the world: "You can have no share in Him, but 'My beloved is mine and I am his' (Song of Songs 2:16), 'I am my beloved's and my beloved is mine,'" etc. (ibid. 6:3). (*Mek. Shirata 3*)

I claim that R. Soloveitchik is suggesting that when faith communities meet, asking them to give up this dimension of the faith experience undermines the very intensity of love and intimacy. This perspective sheds light on his emphasis on exclusivist eschatology. Although we live with this sense of personal intimacy, we can still meet in another realm because we don't live in one existential realm only. Our identities involve a double-confrontation. Our faith experiences are not nurtured only by the exclusivity and uniqueness of the experience of covenantal election. Our religious experience operates with two vocabularies. In the vocabulary of creation we are challenged to build shared meanings, shared frameworks of understanding, and shared experiences of solidarity with all of humanity; the vocabulary of the covenantal election points to the intimacy of love that emphasizes distinctiveness and separateness.

The universal gesture is nurtured by the theme of creation.

It is where we seek to take our own individual faith experience and allow it to enrich our shared human world. In dealing with social, economic, and political concerns, I don't necessarily have to meet you from my own language of intimacy.

In other words, R. Soloveitchik may be understood to mean that in the very intimacy of the life of faith there may be no room for sharing theological faith moments with one who is radically "other," because that intimacy is powered by exclusivity and uniqueness. But there is another realm in which people of faith live, and that is the universal, cosmic confrontation. R. Soloveitchik challenges people of faith to discover an alternative language, one in which moral concerns and social justice are not understood only from the covenantal faith experience but above all from the creational experience, in which each one of us reflects the image of the Creator God. A faith commitment grounded in creation provides people of faith with a universal religious-moral language with which to explore shared goals to alleviate human suffering.

This, I believe, is the essence of R. Soloveitchik's plea to Jews to live with double-confrontation. He wants us to speak in alternative languages; to speak a creational, cosmic language and a covenantal halakhic language. In the former, we step out of Sinai into a reality where I am a creature who shares with all human beings the dignity of having been created in the image of God. In the latter, we speak an intimate covenantal language that is mediated by our particular collective historical consciousness. Both are faith languages, but each is nurtured by its particular theological perspective.

6

PRAYER

R. SOLOVEITCHIK'S DIFFERENT descriptions of the halakhic experience are not always consistent. At times his focus is on human initiative and autonomy, bold new adventures of the spirit, openness to new possibilities, faith in one's capacity to cope with the challenges of human existence. At other times his portrait is much more subdued, reflective, and self-conscious. The optimistic mood gives way to a melancholy spirit marked by doubt and resignation, helpless surrender in terror before the mysterious power of God, and a desperate longing to break out of one's isolation. There are moments when R. Soloveitchik invites you to celebrate the excitement of an existence in which his halakhic man looks upon the world as inviting his creative potential. And yet at other times the universe does not appear as an inviting place, and you find yourself being dragged down by feelings of self-reproach and unworthiness. These oscillations are also powerfully evident in R. Soloveitchik's treatment of prayer.

PRAYER AND COVENANTAL ADEQUACY

The first depiction of the prayer experience is the one we have seen in "The Lonely Man of Faith," which expresses the self-confident assertive posture of R. Soloveitchik's religious anthropology. Here, worshipers do not doubt their own legitimacy or ability to enter the prayer experience. Here, the Jew addresses God as "Thou" and re-lives the covenantal revelatory experience in which God redeems the human being and the community from torturous isolation. God's revelation in history, as distinct from God's manifestation in nature, makes possible the emergence of a new individual and a new community.

On the natural level, existence, as R. Soloveitchik portrays it, is impersonal. The challenge nature poses to the community and to the individual is how to overcome nature's cruel indifference in order to survive. The urgency to survive creates a cooperative human effort to build a society capable of mastering the art of sur-vival. On this cosmic natural level there is cooperation, but love and personal intimacy are absent. To use Martin Buber's language, God, as perceived in nature, creates the relational ontology of "I-It" and not "I-Thou." Only when God directly encounters human beings and is present in personal speech as a Thou does the human being find the resources to go beyond surface communication and to develop those human capacities that enable him or her to be-come what R. Soloveitchik calls an in-depth personality. Only through God's revelation to the human being as a personal being do love and sacrificial action in human relationships become possible.

The covenant at Sinai corresponds to an existential human need to discover love, intimacy, and total commitment in relation-ships. From R. Soloveitchik's religious perspective, the emergence of these human capacities requires God's revelatory presence. They do not come about within human beings through their own efforts, but are made possible when God becomes present in a new way in the human world. It is revelation in history that creates new human potentials for love. Revelation is not a terrifying experience that overwhelms its recipients and reduces them to feelings of insignificance; rather, it is a redeeming and energizing experience. Because of revelation, Adam is no longer shut up within himself, cut off from feelings of love necessary for his fulfillment as a total human personality. God in the revelatory moment transforms the whole framework of interpersonal relational possibilities.

> Only when God emerged from the transcendent darkness of He-anonymity into the illumined spaces of community-knowability and charged man with an ethico-moral mission, did Adam *absconditus* and Eve *abscondita,* while revealing themselves to God in prayer and in unqualified commitment, also reveal themselves to each other in sympathy and love on the one hand and common action on the other. (1965: 45)

From this perspective, the human being's powers of love are energized as a result of encountering God in prayer. Prayer makes it possible for one to become a revealing human being. Adam and Eve, symbolic of all interpersonal human relationships, become transformed human beings, in-depth personalities, when they are addressed by God. God's presence to them as Thou energizes their whole being and enables them to move from a functional utilitarian perspective to a covenantal one. The later generations of biblical history continue this movement. Personal and intimate speech flows from their beings as they participate in the prophetic community of ancient Israel and in the prayer community that becomes institutionalized after the return from Babylonian exile. There is a parallelism between the encounter with God in prayer and the interpersonal encounter on the human plane, and indeed, R.

Soloveitchik's understanding of covenantal prayer and the covenantal faith community is intimately connected to his description of the human condition and of human relationships.

INSTITUTIONALIZED PRAYER AS A CONTINUATION OF PROPHECY

R. Soloveitchik depicts the institution of fixed communal prayer as a conscious response by the Jewish community to the waning and disappearance of prophecy. The Great Assembly organized by Nehemiah and Ezra decided that if God had stopped talking to them in revelation, then they must initiate a continuation of the dialogue through prayer.

> The word of prophecy is God's and is accepted by man. The word of prayer is man's and God accepts it. The two Halakhic traditions tracing the origin of prayer to Abraham and the other Patriarchs and attributing the authorship of statutory prayer to the men of the Great Assembly reveal the Judaic view of the sameness of the prophecy and prayer communities. Covenantal prophecy and prayer blossomed forth the very instant Abraham met God and became involved in a strange colloquy. At a later date, when the mysterious men of this wondrous assembly witnessed the bright summer day of the prophetic community full of color and sound turning to a bleak autumnal night of dreadful silence unilluminated by the vision of God or made homely by His voice, they refused to acquiesce in this cruel historical reality and would not let the ancient dialogue between God and men come to an end. . . . In prayer they found the salvation of the colloquy,

which, they insisted, must go on forever. If God had stopped calling man, they urged, let man call God. So the covenantal colloquy was shifted from the level of prophecy to that of prayer. (1965: 36–37)

The men of the Great Assembly's refusal to allow the absence of God's revelatory word to be a permanent feature of history, their refusal to acquiesce in God's silence in history, speaks volumes for their felt sense of adequacy and their awareness that they were playing an essential role in maintaining the ongoing intimacy and dialogue between God and Israel. They knew that God must be present in a personal, intimate way with the community. They refused to admit the possibility that with the end of prophecy the passionate intimate dialogue between God and Israel had come to an end. If God stops speaking to Israel through prophets, then it is time for human beings to take the initiative in the dialogue between God and Israel. The absence of revelation and of overt miraculous divine involvement in history did not drive them into feelings of self-doubt, terror, inadequacy, and rejection. It is interesting to note R. Soloveitchik's use of the expression "they refused to acquiesce" in explaining their response of initiating statutory prayer, as if God were not free to choose whether or not to be present among them. The response of the men of the Great Assembly defines God's continuous presence in the life of community.

This understanding of how prayer developed is similar in spirit to the following talmudic discussion of the statement in the Mishnah:

[Mishnah] All who have incurred [the penalty of] kareth, on being flogged obtain remission from their punishment of kareth; for it is said, forty he shall have him beaten, he shall not exceed . . . lest thy brother shall be dishonoured before thine eyes, which shows that on having received the flogging he is [considered] "thy brother": these are the words of R. Hananiah B. Gamaliel.

[Gemara] Said R. Joseph: Who has gone up [to Heaven] and come [back with this information]?—Said Abaye to him: But then, in regard to what R. Joshua b. Levi said: "Three things were enacted by the [mundane] Tribunal below, and the Celestial Tribunal on high have given assent to their action; [we might also exclaim,] who has gone up [to Heaven] and come [back with this information]? Only, we [obtain these points by] interpreting certain texts; and, in this instance too, we so interpret the texts." (*b. Makkot* 23a, b)

Karet is a punishment meted out by God. Nevertheless, the Mishnah claims that a person who receives *makot* (lashes) is exempt from the divine punishment of *karet*. The Talmud then asks how a rabbinic interpreter could know how God will act in a situation where the sinner is guilty of *karet*. The answer given is that rabbinic authority to interpret biblical texts is similar to their "authority" to decide how God will respond to violations of the law. The discussion in the Talmud presupposes that we can understand God, that we may even be so bold as to define, in certain circumstances, the way God will or possibly must act.

The full and total self-confidence as to what God requires of human beings grows from knowledge of and devotion to the text of the Torah. Just as the rabbis are competent to introduce new legislation defining how the community is to behave, so too can they define how God will act with the sinner. The intellectual mastery of the word of God in the Torah is all that the scholar requires to understand and to define how both members of the covenant, God and the community of Israel, are to behave.

Israel as a convenantal learning community defines how the divine word is appropriated and understood in history. Just as they are competent to define the consequences and scope of revelation, they are equally competent to decide how God's presence is manifest in community. Prayer reflects the confident and bold spirit of the covenantal community that insists on maintaining a continuous intimate dialogue with God.

For R. Soloveitchik, there is a threefold covenantal connection between the prayer and prophetic communities. To begin with, the paradigm for prayer in "The Lonely Man of Faith" is the face-to-face encounter of God with Moses. It is the speech of a friend. It is the speech of a prophet who feels adequate and dignified in the encounter with God. There is no dread and awe of the numinous.

> Only within the covenantal community which is formed by God descending upon the mountain and man, upon the call of the Lord, ascending the mount is a direct and personal relationship expressing itself in the prophetic "face to face" colloquy established. "And the Lord spoke unto Moses face to face as man speaketh unto his friend." (1965: 34)

It is this biblical description (Exod. 33:11) of the face-to-face encounter between God and Moses that R. Soloveitchik wants his readers to focus upon as he relates prayer to the prophetic experience. The universe in which the prophetic and prayer communities live invites the personal encounter between the human being and God. The essence of prayer is the existential awareness that one lives in the presence of God in a personal and intimate way and that the divine presence can be addressed through direct and warm speech. This is the covenantal God whose name is the Tetragrammaton. Reflection on the impersonal God of nature, designated by the term "Elohim," does not lead to prayer, because the essence of prayer for R. Soloveitchik is relational intimacy.

> The cosmic drama, notwithstanding its grandeur and splendor, no matter how distinctly it reflects the image of the Creator and no matter how beautifully it tells His glory, cannot provoke man to prayer. (1965: 35)

Only the framework of prophetic revelation makes prayer as personal encounter possible. Prayer as the continuation of the prophetic experience must not, therefore, be confused with the formal objective form of institutional prayer. The language in which prayer is cast and the elaborate rituals the Halakhah requires are formal means for expressing the encounter with God as a personal Thou.

The overwhelming awareness of being in the presence of God constitutes, for R. Soloveitchik, the essence and soul of the prayer experience. The recitation of the words of prayer without this profound consciousness empties prayer of religious significance.

> Prayer is basically an awareness of man finding himself in the presence of and addressing himself to his Maker, and to pray has one connotation only: to stand before God. To be sure, this awareness has been objectified and crystallized in standardized, definitive texts whose recitation is obligatory . . . —it remains unalterably true that the very essence of prayer is the covenantal experience of being together with and talking to God and that the concrete performance such as the recitation of texts represents the technique of implementation of prayer and not prayer itself. (1965: 35)

R. Soloveitchik's distinction between "the very essence of prayer" and the concrete performance that represents "the technique of implementation of prayer and not prayer itself" is crucial for understanding his philosophy of prayer and Halakhah.

Though Halakhah characteristically translates inner feelings and attitudes into concrete action, there remains an interaction in Halakhah between formal, external performance and subjective fulfillment. In halakhic terminology, prayer entails a potential split between *ma'aseh ha-mitzvah*, the act of the commandment (in this case, the utterance of prescribed words at prescribed times), and *kiyum ha-mitzvah*, the complete fulfillment of the commandment, which includes the subjective intention that must inform the articulation of formal prayers. The *kiyum she be'lev*, the inner fulfillment of the norm, necessitates a devotional attitude even though the *ma'aseh*, the act per se, is external and public. There are other *mitzvot*, such as eating *matzah* (unleavened bread) on Passover, where, to many halakhists, the absence of proper intention does not invalidate the fulfillment of the halakhic norm in question (in accordance with the principle "*Mitzvot* do not necessarily require *kavvanah* [intention])." But prayer is void of meaning unless accompanied by a particular devotional attitude.

The popular Biblical term *tefillah* and the esoteric halakhic term *avodah shebelev* refer to an inner activity, to a state of mind. *Kavvanah*, related to prayer is, unlike the *kavvanah* concerning other *mitzvah* performances, not an extraneous addendum but the very core of prayer. The whole Halakhic controversy about *kavvanah* vis-à-vis other *mitzvot* has no relevance to prayer. There is not a single opinion that the latter can be divorced from *kavvanah*. Moreover, the substance of *kavvanah* as far as prayer is concerned differs fundamentally from that which some require during the performance of other *mitzvot.* While the former denotes a state of mind, an all-embracing awareness of standing before the Almighty, the latter manifests itself only in the normative intention on the part of the *mitzvah*-doer to act in accordance with the will of God. *Kavvanah* in both cases, of course, expresses direction or aiming. However, in prayer, one must direct his whole self toward God whereas in the case of other *mitzvot* the directing is confined to a single act. (1965: 35–36 n)

The objective forms of prayer are given technical importance because of the concern for the community and the democratization of Judaism. But they do not touch on the essence of the experience of prayer, which is the awareness of standing in the presence of God.

A second feature that prophecy and prayer share is commitment to the community. Prophecy from a Jewish perspective is not a private ecstatic experience. The prophet brings an urgent normative message from a God who seeks to be embodied in the life of the community. The prophetic experience does not isolate the prophet from the community but places the prophet in a matrix of social and political action. Prayer reflects this same pattern, as is shown by the plural form present in all the petitional prayers. In Judaic prayer one never prays for oneself alone, but always begins by praying on behalf of the community with a prayer whose style is "Heal *us*, redeem *us*, restore Thy *people* to Jerusalem." As one stands before God, the drama of Jewish history and the urgent need of the total community are engraved in one's consciousness. As the prayer consciousness fills the heart of the worshiper, preoccupation with self falls away and is replaced by solidarity with the needs of others and an awareness that one's being is inextricably linked to the destiny of one's community.

This commitment to the community leads to a third feature shared by the prayer and prophetic communities. Both the prophet and the praying individual recognize the centrality of ethical action in their covenantal experience with God.

> When confronted with God, the prophet receives an ethico-moral message to be handed down to and realized by the members of the covenantal community which is mainly a community in action. . . . Prayer likewise consists not only of an awareness of the presence of God, but of an act of committing oneself to God and accepting His ethico-moral authority. . . . Prayer is always the harbinger of moral reformation. (1965: 39–42)

Prayer is here defined as a prologue to practice. Its essence, which is drawn from the covenantal encounter, is to awaken the worshiper to the centrality of acting with justice in the world. As the continuation of the prophetic encounter, prayer casts the individual into social action. It is not resignation, helplessness, or withdrawal. It is not quietism or a relinquishment of personal responsibility. For R. Soloveitchik, prayer as encounter, as discovery of God as Thou, is consummated only in moral action. In prayer the powers of love and solidarity become so intense that the prayerful individual must become an active being within the social and political reality.

PRAYER AND SELF-DISCOVERY

The classic prayer in the Judaic tradition is the Amidah, the standing, silent devotional prayer consisting of three benedictions of praise, thirteen of petition, and three of thanksgiving. The Talmud (*Berakhot* 34a) sees this structure as mirroring the way a humble servant would supplicate a master. It is not appropriate, according to the rabbis, to begin immediately with one's needs. A servant first gives words of praise to the master and only then petitions for personal needs. After presenting these petitions, the servant offers thanksgiving. However, the fundamental driving force in approaching the master remains need and dependency. The praise and thanksgiving are ways of giving one's petition a respectful aesthetic form.

In R. Soloveitchik's essay "Redemption, Prayer, Talmud Torah," petitional prayer is interpreted as a process of self-discovery. In learning how to utter petitional prayer, people are transformed from mute beings, unable to articulate their pains and needs, into dignified beings who can express them in meaningful linguistic structures. Judaic prayer began when "the children of Israel sighed by reason of their bondage and their cry came up to God" (Exod. 2:23), but it reaches maturity only when the outpouring of human needs is subjected to the discipline of the mind in the Amidah.

> In the final stage, the word appears; the outcry is transformed into speech. Man, at this level, not only feels his needs but understands them as well; there is a logic of prayer which opens up to man when he is in possession of the word. . . . The hierarchy of needs, clearly defined and evaluated, is to be found in the text of the Amidah, where not only the emotional need-awareness, but also the logos of need and with it the human being himself are redeemed. The outpouring of the heart merges with the insights of the mind. To pray means to discriminate, to evaluate, to understand, in other words, to ask intelligently. I pray for the gratification of some needs since I consider them worthy of being gratified. I refrain from petitioning God for the

satisfaction of other wants because it will not enhance my dignity. (1978d: 66–67)

To use R. Soloveitchik's terms (1978d: 70), this experience of petitional prayer leads toward the pole of self-acquisition, self-discovery, self-objectification, self-redemption. The focus is not on how God will respond to the words uttered in prayer but on how those words change the human being. R. Soloveitchik regards human beings as discovering their human essence when they are able to comprehend and articulate the fundamental needs that define the proper aspirations of humankind. Halakhic prayer emphasizes petition, which articulates the human being's proper needs, because it is crucial not to be confused as to what is an essential human need. To misunderstand those needs is to misunderstand the essence of being human. From this posture, the mood of prayer is philosophic and analytic and close to the reflective learning experience found in *Halakhic Man*.

THE SECOND VIEW: PETITIONAL PRAYER AND SELF-SACRIFICE

R. Soloveitchik ends "Redemption, Prayer, Talmud Torah," however, with a sudden dialectical leap toward the opposite pole. Having led us to self-acquisition, prayer requires from us total self-sacrifice.

> Judaic dialectic plays "mischievously" with two opposites, two irreconcilable aspects of prayer. It announces prayer as self-acquisition, self-discovery, self-objectification and self-redemption. . . . Yet there is another aspect to prayer: prayer is an act of giving away. Prayer means

sacrifice, unrestricted offering of the whole self, the returning to God of body and soul, everything one possesses and cherishes. (1978d: 70)

R. Soloveitchik offers no explanation for this unexpected complete shift of direction, apart from the different connotations of the word *avodah:* "sacrifice" as well as "worship" and "service." To understand his intention, we must turn to other writings, especially his Hebrew essay "Ra'ayonot al ha-Tefillah," where prayer and specifically the Amidah are characterized without any emphasis on human dignity and assertion. In contrast to "The Lonely Man of Faith," "Ra'ayonot al ha-Tefillah" presents the *akedah* (the binding of Isaac) rather than covenantal intimacy as the dominant paradigm for understanding prayer.

Petitional prayer, rather than being a vehicle leading to self-discovery or expressing human solidarity and commitment to the well-being of others, is understood now as self-sacrifice. Worship of the heart, which finds its fullest expression in the middle petitional benedictions, does not lead to the humanizing encounter with God as the eternal Thou, but is now total surrender to the awesome terror of divinity. It is an act of sacrifice, an act of casting oneself down before the Lord and acknowledging the unlimited rule of the divine and the complete feebleness of humankind. In petitional prayer, we urgently seek out God's grace and help because we are overwhelmed by feelings of insignificance and helplessness.

R. Soloveitchik prefers the Hebrew word *tehinnah* to *bakkashah* as the appropriate term for petitional prayer because *bakkashah,* the customary term, suggests a claim upon God, whereas *tehinnah* etymologically "suggests an unearned grace, something not due to us." Nonetheless, he explains, *tehinnah* is emphasized in Judaism because the emotion of dependence and helplessness is singled out above all others as the central existential posture of worship. The feeling of wretchedness is paramount for authentic prayer.

For R. Soloveitchik, the sacrificial gesture of prayer is not reflected only in the thirteen petitional benedictions. He discovers the most exalted petition in the opening benediction of the third section of the Amidah, which states,

> Be pleased, Lord our God, with Thy people Israel and with their prayer. Restore the worship to Thy most holy sanctuary. Accept Israel's offering and prayer with gracious love, and may the worship of Thy people Israel be ever pleasing to Thee.

R. Soloveitchik understands the words "Accept Israel's offering and prayer with gracious love" as an offering of the self to God (1979b: 268–69). The whole Amidah, in fact, is seen as a declaration of the human being's utter insignificance and helplessness before God, thereby signifying the total sacrifice to God of one's own being.

The worshiper's consciousness of total dependency is not derived only from social, political, and economic needs. For R. Soloveitchik, it is ontological. Prayer as self-sacrifice touches upon the very legitimacy of human existence and the very essence of what it means to be a finite creature before God. Its paradigm is the *akedah*, the binding of Isaac.

> Build an altar. Arrange the pieces of wood. Kindle the fire. Take the knife to slaughter your existence for My sake thus commands the awe-some God Who suddenly appears from absolute seclusion. This approach is the basis of prayer. Man surrenders himself to God. He approaches the awesome God and the approach

expresses itself in the sacrifice and Akedah of oneself.
(1979b: 255)

PRAYER AND DREAD

In this second paradigm of prayer, too, R. Soloveitchik connects
rabbinic prayer to the prophetic biblical experience. However, in
"Ra'ayonot al ha-Tefillah" the portrait of the prophetic experience
is radically different from that found in "The Lonely Man of
Faith." Gone is the emphasis on Moses' "friendly" face-to-face encounter with God, with the ease and acceptance that characterized
it. The prophetic experience is now in no way analogous to the interpersonal relationship of friendship and love. Instead, R. Soloveitchik calls upon biblical texts that emphasize the terror and awe
felt in the prophetic encounter with God.

R. Soloveitchik's paradigm is now not Moses' face-to-face
encounter with God, but a Moses who hides his face because he is
afraid to look at God in the burning bush, a Moses who is told,
"You cannot see My face because no man can see My face and live"
(Exod. 33:20). R. Soloveitchik deliberately selects those biblical
descriptions that bring home to his readers the enormous terror
that fills the heart of a human being who encounters the presence
of God. Prayer as continuing the prophetic experience takes on a
radically new meaning when it is the prophet's terror before God
that is portrayed.

In "Ra'ayonot al ha-Tefillah" the covenantal community's
experience at Sinai is an awesome, terrifying experience in which
human finitude is overwhelmed in the encounter with divinity.
When it meets the infinite, the finite human being, says R. Soloveitchik, must lose all sense of ontological legitimacy and dignity.
It is therefore no wonder that the people are terrified and
awestruck at the revelatory moment of Sinai and cry out to Moses

to act as their mediator. Revelation, rather than confirming dignity, creates the terror of death: "All the people witnessed the thunder and lightning, the blare of the horn and the mountain smoking; and when the people saw it they fell back and stood at a distance. 'You speak to us,' they said to Moses, 'and we will obey. But let not God speak to us lest we die'" (Exod. 20:18–19). For R. Soloveitchik, this dread is what every individual should feel who dares approach God in prayer.

> The Halakhah never let its attention be distracted from an aspect [of prayer] which constituted for it an almost insoluble problem and an amazing paradox. In the eyes of the sages of the tradition, having recourse to God in speech and entreaty seemed a bold and adventurous action. How can mortal man, who is here today and in the grave tomorrow, approach the King of the kings of kings, the Holy One, blessed be He? Can we say that permission is given to a common person to talk to a high and exalted King and to request his needs from Him?
>
> Evidently, the experience of fear and trembling, which is an integral part of the religious life, complicates the problem of prayer and turns it into a marvelous riddle. On the one hand, it is impossible for man to approach God. To the extent that man approaches God, his finite human existence is contradicted. Finitude is swallowed up in infinity and expires in its recesses. . . . The personality and self-confidence of man are as nothing in comparison with the majesty of God and the splendor of His glory. The question bursts out: how is it possible for prayer to exist? (1979b: 244)

According to R. Soloveitchik, the agonizing dialectic between the desperate necessity of prayer and the total unworthiness of human beings to pray accompanies the worshiper throughout the whole Amidah experience. Already in the rabbinic period, the Amidah was prefixed by the verse "O Lord, open Thou my lips and my mouth shall declare Thy praise" (Ps. 51:15). R. Soloveitchik's ideal worshiper, when pronouncing this introductory sentence, is filled with anxiety over the virtual impossibility of prayer and is begging God for help to utter any words at all.

> One who comes to begin entreating and petitioning [God] is full of fear: his initial immediate reaction expresses itself in paralyzing terror and alarmed trembling. He asks himself: how is it possible to conduct a conversation between man and his Creator? As his lips move, he expresses with quivering and trembling his weakness and insignificance. He begins saying: "O Lord, open Thou my lips and my mouth shall declare Thy praise." That is to say: "I do not know how to move my lips and find suitable words in order to express my thoughts. God, do that for me. I entreat Thee not only about the fulfillment of my petitions and the supply of my needs, but about the matter of the prayer itself. Foolish I am and I know nothing." This is the general introduction. A confession of dejection about his baseness, his distress, and his despair. See, he is entreating the Holy One, blessed be He: "Teach me how to pray." (1979b: 248–49)

There is an internal conflict in the soul of this worshiper. On the one hand, prayer is urgent and necessary. The worshiper's religious life would be sapped of all its vitality if one could not pour out one's deepest needs and feelings before God. Yet, on the other hand, the mere human being is terrified, frightened, and overwhelmed by the reality of God. How dare we presume that God can be approached? It is this haunting sense of unworthiness that underlies the introductory quest for God to help one to pray.

Since this inner contradiction weighs so heavily on the worshiper, the first benediction of the Amidah tries to reassure us that we are welcome before God.

> Blessed art Thou, O Lord, our God and God of our fathers, the God of Abraham, the God of Isaac, and the God of Jacob, the great, the mighty, and the awesome God, the most high God, who bestows abundant grace, and creates all things, and remembers the gracious deeds of [Himself to] the fathers, and will bring a Redeemer to their children's children for His name's sake out of love. O King, Supporter, Savior, and Shield: blessed art Thou, O Lord, the Shield of Abraham.

From terror the worshiper moves to feelings of acceptance, sensing God's abundant grace as mirrored in the creation of nature. The first benediction, which recalls God's relationship to the patriarchs, mediates for the worshiper the way Abraham discovered God's wisdom and love, in the structure of being. The worshiper who utters the words "the God of Abraham, the God of Isaac, and the God of Jacob" is inspired with feelings of divine acceptance. It is for this reason that the words *melekh ha-olam,* "King of the Universe," do not appear in the first benediction of the Amidah. R. Soloveitchik claims that the intimacy of God's love in this benediction precludes focusing on God's majestic glory. The patriarchs, who found God in nature, bring God's overflowing grace to the consciousness of the worshiper.

In "Ra'ayonot al ha-Tefillah" the God of revelation inspires terror and silence. It is the God of nature who liberates the human being and creates prayer as a vital living possibility. Creation is the carrier of love, revelation the carrier of terror. But creation does not give legitimacy to the worshiper in his or her own right. Only the worshiper who participates in prayer as a member of a historical covenantal community can stand before God. "On his own he who prays is worth nothing; together with the generations he reflects the image of the father of the generations: Abraham!" (1979b: 249). Although nature mirrors God's overflowing love to every single individual, for R. Soloveitchik, prayer is possible only through participation in the covenantal community of Abraham.

R. Soloveitchik, however, expects a great change of mood in the worshiper who passes from recalling God's love and acceptance to the second benediction, which describes the power of God and the utter helplessness and insignificance of the human being. "Pride sinks down and humility springs up" (1979b: 256). The mood of self-negation and terror acquires even greater intensity as the worshiper pronounces the third and last of the benedictions of praise: "Thou art holy and Thy name is holy, and holy ones praise Thee every day. Blessed art Thou, O Lord, the holy God." When worshipers are conscious of God as holy, trepidation fills their hearts. They are prepared to sacrifice everything to God (1979b: 257).

For R. Soloveitchik, God excused the Israelites from sacrificing their *bodies* on the altar, but expected them to understand that in bringing an animal sacrifice they were vicariously bringing their total personality as a sacrifice before God.

> With regard to the sacrifice as an experience the Holy One, blessed be He, demands a human sacrifice. Sacrificing an animal is only a symbolic act. The chief correlative of the external act is a spiritual act of offering a soul in sacrifice. . . . The Akedah of Isaac, which occupies such an important place in the liturgy and worldview of Israel, signifies: the Akedah and sacrifice of a man. The law of sacrifices demands a human

sacrifice clothed in the form of an animal. (1979b: 254–55)

After the destruction of the Second Temple, animal sacrifices were no longer possible. Petitional prayer then became the vehicle through which the spirit of human self-sacrifice continued as a live religious experience. Today, Jewish prayer contains a sacrificial dimension when petitioning worshipers acknowledge total dependency and helplessness before God, that only God is mighty and not they, that God is holy and they are but dust and ashes (1979b: 256).

PRAYER AND PRECEDENT

According to R. Soloveitchik, it is because human beings are so insignificant and helpless before God that they are dependent upon precedent to dare to pray at all. For that reason, R. Soloveitchik considered it presumptuous to make the slightest change in the forms of prayer. The three fixed daily prayers—morning, afternoon, and evening—are all that are permitted to a Jew. This excluded not only the innovations introduced in Reform Jewish worship, but even spontaneous voluntary prayer.

Since it is only the distant past that legitimates prayer today, there must be absolute commitment and conformity to the prayer forms of the tradition. In utilizing the fixed forms of the tradition, the worshiper admits his or her unworthiness to pray. The words of the prayer book are a gift of the tradition—it is permissible to approach God in prayer because my ancestors prayed. By submitting to the prayer forms that the tradition has given me, I both acknowledge the absolute urgency to stand in prayer before God and confess my sense of personal unworthiness to do so.

R. Soloveitchik does not portray the absolute authority of

the traditional forms of prayer as crushing human poetic passion and creativity. Rather, the willing renunciation of innovative or spontaneous prayer expresses the heroic self-sacrificial feature of R. Soloveitchik's dialectical anthropology. Jews submit to the halakhic form of prayer because of the existential terror that finite human beings feel before the infinite God, not because Judaism enslaves one to the past.

The existential characterology of self-negation is also used, in "Prayer as Dialogue," to justify opposition to the customs in modern Reform and Conservative synagogues of allowing men and women to sit together, as opposed to the Orthodox practice of gender separation in the synagogue.

> Out of this sense of discomfiture prayer emerges. Offered in comfort and security, prayer is a paradox, modern methods of suburban worship and plush synagogues notwithstanding. The desire for proximity of wife and children at services comes from a need for security and comfort. Real prayer is derived from loneliness, helplessness, and a sense of dependence. (1979a: 81)

In "Ra'ayonot al ha-Tefillah" there is no place for free, spontaneous prayer in R. Soloveitchik's approach to prayer. *Tefillat nedavah*, prayer that is a free, spontaneous gift, would presuppose that God is easily approachable. Only one who feels welcome to stand before God could look upon *tefillat nedavah* as a legitimate form of prayer. For R. Soloveitchik, however, there is no one alive today who is qualified to act in that spirit. Individuals can pray only as the children's children of the patriarchs, whose unique ability to initiate prayer was consolidated by the scribes and sages of the tradition. Only within the ordered framework of ritual prayer is one given the legitimacy to express petitional needs. Any outpouring of the soul that is not grounded in total subordination to rabbinic liturgical forms must be viewed as egocentric expressions of an arrogant individual who has forgotten that prayer is a gift from the tradition and that the individual may approach God only because of the historical precedent set by the patriarchs.

> The worshiper does not have permission to ask for his own needs. An egoistic supplication which falls outside the form of prayer that was instituted by the men of the Great Assembly is forbidden. (1979b: 267)

For R. Soloveitchik, the modern Jew is able to stand before God only by dint of being a remote descendant of those who received the Torah at Sinai. In his view, the covenantal community, which extends across generations, redeems the individual Jew from an existence that is fundamentally worthless and empty of significance. It keeps us from being overwhelmed and crushed by a divine reality that seems to repulse human beings and negate their right to approach God in prayer. We must use the absolutely immutable forms of Judaic prayer, according to R. Soloveitchik, because we can pray only as tiny components of a vast historical drama, not as contemporary individuals with our own sentiments and concerns. If we dare step outside the fixed structure and language of prayer handed down by the tradition, we lose the right to speak. In contrast to the meaning R. Soloveitchik ascribes to the formal linguistic institutionalization of the Amidah prayer in "The Lonely Man of Faith," in "Ra'ayonot al ha-Tefillah" the objective form is given enormous religious significance because it expresses the dread, awe, and sense of total insignificance that overcome the individual in the moment of prayer.

A CRITICAL EVALUATION OF
PRAYER AS SELF-SACRIFICE

The bold, assertive actions of the patriarchs, the prophets, and the men of the Great Assembly with respect to prayer are unique exceptions, unique both in the history of Israel and even in the lives of the persons concerned. Hence the manner in which R. Soloveitchik employs them as precedents: later generations are not endowed with the ability to act in the spirit of Abraham, Moses, or Ezra in those founding moments of covenantal history.

I am critical of this approach to prayer because it does not do justice to the idea that the Sinai covenant is renewed in each generation. God said to Abraham, "I will establish My covenant between Me and you and your generations for an everlasting covenant" (Gen. 17:7). Creativity, adequacy, and boldness of spirit were not permitted by God only to those who participated in the founding covenantal moments; rather, they define the ongoing vitality of the eternal covenant between God and God's human partners in every generation. They are essential features of a life lived in the spirit of a constantly reaffirmed covenant. "I make this covenant, with its sanctions, not with you alone, but both with those who are standing here with us this day before the Lord our God and with those who are not with us here this day" (Deut. 29:13–14).

The men of the Great Assembly described in "The Lonely Man of Faith" were not burdened by R. Soloveitchik's antinomies when they decided to introduce statutory prayer as a natural expression of covenantal intimacy. The patriarchs were not crushed by self-doubt when they approached God in prayer. Their covenantal consciousness, imbued with a sense of God's irrevocable love and acceptance, are a permanent feature of covenantal anthropology. As R. Soloveitchik himself argues in *Halakhic Man*, one cannot separate God's covenantal commandments from God's acceptance of those commanded. One cannot separate a human life defined by covenantal mitzvot from its implied anthropology.

R. Soloveitchik supports the motif of self-sacrifice in prayer by focusing on the prophet's terror before God and viewing that as paradigmatic for the way that we should feel when we pray. This identification of prayer with the rare moments of prophetic experience cannot serve as a model of daily prayer. The astonishment of Moses at the burning bush and the terror of the community at Mount Sinai have not been constant experiential features of the religious life of Israel. They were unique intense moments in which an individual or a community was enveloped by a very singular overwhelming manifestation of God. Such experiences do not represent the norm of what it means to live in covenantal relationship with God.

Prayer can be understood, as Yeshayahu Leibowitz claimed, as an integral part of a total way of life organized by mitzvah. As R. Soloveitchik repeatedly argues, mitzvah mediates God's commanding will and presence in everyday life. In insisting that the community observe the mitzvot, Judaism taught both that human beings can fulfill the divine commandments and that they have no need to feel overwhelmed, terrified, and awestruck by the divine presence when it is mediated by the commanding will present in mitzvot. For one committed to mitzvot, this is a normal perception of everyday reality. Just as one regularly fulfills the mitzvot without terror, so also one prays regularly without terror, since prayer is part of the mitzvah life. This is not to deny that there are possibly moments of enormous religious intensity within the prayer experience. However, they are not paradigmatic for the way one stands before God in prayer, any more than for the way one fulfills God's will in performing the different mitzvot. As Moshe Greenberg shows, biblical prayer is rooted not exclusively in moments of ecstasy or terror, but rather, in the everyday experience of members of the community. It is "the popular life of prayer" that enables the community to be receptive to the prophetic message."[10]

Prayer is related to the normative experience of Judaism in which we live before God without being overwhelmed and terrified. It mirrors the normal religious consciousness of the believer in a personal God. The exalted rank of the prophet or the ecstasy of the mystic is not a precondition for feeling invited to participate in the prayer experience. The covenant was given to the whole community and was also meant for the most ordinary member of the community in the most elementary situations of life. Judaism as a total way of life for a whole community sets the grounds for the prayer encounter. When the community turns from its daily activities to its daily prayer, it is not expected to make a leap from the prosaic to the ecstatic, but to express and clarify in words what its covenantal relationship with God signifies in its way of life. The relational intimacy of prayer grows out of the normative life of Judaism; it is not its antithesis.

PRAYER AND GOD CONSCIOUSNESS

In "Ra'ayonot al ha-Tefillah" R. Soloveitchik refers to Maimonides as the redeemer of prayer because Maimonides established prayer as a Torah-grounded commandment (*mitzvah min ha-torah*) and not, as Nachmanides claimed, a rabbinic commandment. An examination of Maimonides' writings on prayer reveals a different perspective on prayer than what R. Soloveitchik claims in "Ra'ayonot al ha-Tefillah." In the *Mishneh Torah*, Maimonides describes the commandment of prayer as follows:

---

[10]Moshe Greenberg, *Biblical Prose Prayer* (Berkeley: University of California Press, 1983), 57.

To pray daily is an affirmative duty, as it is said, "And ye shall serve the Lord, your God" (Exodus 23:25). The service, here referred to according to the teaching of tradition, is Prayer. . . . The number of prayers is not prescribed in the Torah. No form of prayer is prescribed in the Torah. Nor does the Torah prescribe a fixed time for Prayer. . . .

The obligation in this precept is that every person should daily, according to his ability, offer up supplication and prayer; first uttering praises of God, then, with humble supplication and petition ask for all that he needs, and finally offer praise and thanksgiving to the Eternal for the benefits already bestowed upon him in such measure.

One who was fluent would offer up many prayers and supplications. If one was slow of speech, he would pray as he could and whenever he pleased. Thus also, the number of separate services depended on an individual's ability. One would pray once daily; others, several times in the day. All, however, turned during prayer to the Sanctuary, in whichever direction that might be. This was the uniform practice from the times of Moses to those of Ezra. (*M.T. Laws of Prayer* 1:1–3)

According to Maimonides, from the biblical period onwards, individuals offered as many prayers as they desired. The commandment was to pray a minimum of once a day. However, this was not the maximum limit, because, as Maimonides emphasized, individuals would pray whenever they wanted. This implies that there was a total sense of freedom and ease to express oneself before God. And this situation prevailed from Moses until Ezra.

What reasons does Maimonides offer for the change from

freely expressed, individually oriented prayer to the fixed language and format established by the men of the Great Assembly?

> When the people of Israel went into exile in the days of the wicked Nebucednezzar, they mingled with the Persians, Greeks and other nations. In those foreign countries, children were born to them, whose language was confused. Everyone's speech was a mixture of many tongues. No one was able, when he spoke, to express his thoughts adequately in any one language, otherwise than incoherently, as it is said, "And their children spoke half in the speech of Ashdod and they could not speak in the Jews' language, but according to the language of each people" (Nehemiah 13:24).
>
> Consequently, when any one of them prayed in Hebrew, he was unable adequately to express his needs or recount the praises of God, without mixing Hebrew with other languages. When Ezra and his Council realized this condition, they ordained the Eighteen Benedictions in their present order.
>
> The first three blessings consist of praises of God and the last three, of thanksgiving to Him. The intermediate benedictions are petitions for the things which may stand as categories of all the desires of the individual and the needs of the community. (*M.T. Laws of Prayer* 1:4)

The fixed language of prayer liberated individuals from feeling inhibited to approach God because of their incapacity to express themselves fluently in one language. The purpose of fixed formulas was to make the prayer experience available to the whole community and not only to exceptional individuals. It is clear that for Maimonides, institutional prayer was not meant to crush individual spontaneity, but rather, to make God more approachable and accessible to the community at large.

The motif of God's approachability continues in Maimonides' codification of *tefillat nedavah* (voluntary prayer).

> The number of these services may not be diminished but may be increased. If a person wishes to pray the whole day, he may do so. And the prayers he adds are accounted to him as if he brought free-will offerings. He must accordingly add in each of the middle blessings a thought appropriate to the particular blessing. If this is done in one of the blessings only, that is sufficient, the object being to make it manifest that the prayer is voluntary and not obligatory. (*M.T. Laws of Prayer* 1:9)

The institutionalization of obligatory prayer was not meant to limit the individual's right to approach God. This idea is expressed not only in the *Mishneh Torah,* but also in Maimonides' discussion of contemplative prayer in the *Guide for the Perplexed.*

> If, however, you have apprehended God and His acts in accordance with what is required by the intellect, you should afterwards engage in totally devoting yourself to Him, endeavour to come closer to Him, and strengthen the bond between you and Him—that is, the intellect. . . . The Torah has made it clear that this last worship to which we have drawn attention in this chapter can only be engaged in after apprehension has been achieved; it says: *To love the Lord your God, and to serve Him with all your heart and with all your soul.* Now we have made it clear several times that love is proportionate to apprehension. After *love* comes this worship to which attention

195

has also been drawn by [the Sages], *may their memory be blessed,* who said: *This is the worship in the heart.* (*Guide for the Perplexed* 3:51)

Contemplative prayer, which Maimonides calls *avodah she b'lev,* the worship of the heart, is not defined by legal precedent, by the sacrificial motif, or by any specific halakhic regulation, but by the philosopher's natural yearning to meditate upon God's wisdom as manifest throughout the cosmos. *Avodah she b'lev,* in Maimonides' halakhic and philosophical works both, is not the "*offering* of the heart" (Soloveitchik 1978d: 70), in the sense of self-sacrifice, but rather, the yearning to be in the presence of God. Neither the *Mishneh Torah* nor the *Guide for the Perplexed* reflects the existential antinomies, self-doubt, and self-sacrificial motifs that R. Soloveitchik develops in his analysis of prayer. And yet, for R. Soloveitchik, Maimonides is the "redeemer of prayer."

If Maimonides is the great halakhist who confirmed the central importance of prayer in Judaism, it hardly seems plausible for R. Soloveitchik to have developed a religious anthropology that is antithetical to the one presupposed by Maimonides' understanding of prayer. For Maimonides, the freedom and spontaneity of prayer that began with Moses in the biblical period was never lost, but rather, was retained even when prayer was given a structured form by the men of the Great Assembly. The individual's prerogative to worship independently of the fixed legislated structures of worship remained a permanent feature of Judaism.

Besides the apparent internal inconsistency of R. Soloveitchik's approach to the religious dimension of prayer, the traditional texts he cites as precedents for his interpretation are not convincing. In many cases, they suggest a posture to worship that differs from the one he himself proposes.

Although the Babylonian Talmud establishes a connection between the times of the sacrifices and of prayer, it does not imply that the sacrifices determine the content and spirit of the daily Amidah. The Talmud (*Berakhot* 26b) traces the three daily prayers to the patriarchs and uses the precedent of the daily sacrifices in the Temple to define the exact hours when daily prayers should be recited. In the daily Amidah, only the seventeenth benediction, where one prays for the restoration of the Temple and its forms of worship, refers to the sacrificial theme. Only in the additional prayers for the Sabbath, new moon, and festivals is the motif of the sacrificial cult emphasized.

In this passage from the Babylonian Talmud, the rabbis indeed make it clear that the sacrificial motif is not the ultimate ground of daily prayer.

> The question was raised: if a man erred and did not say the afternoon prayer, should he say it twice in the evening? Should you argue from the fact that if he erred in the evening he prays twice in the morning? [I may reply that] this is because it is all one day, as it is written: "And there was evening and there was morning, one day" [Gen. 1:5]. But in this case, prayer being in the place of sacrifice, since the day has passed, the sacrifice lapses. Or should we rather say that since prayer is supplication for mercy, a man may go on praying as long as he likes? Come and hear: for Rabbi Hunah ben Judah said in the name of Rabbi Isaac reporting Rabbi Johanan: "If a man erred and did not say the afternoon prayer, he says it twice in the evening and we do not apply here the principle that if the day has passed, the offering lapses." (*b. Berakhot* 26a)

The theme of prayer as supplication for mercy (*rahamim*) overrides the theme of prayer as a substitute for daily sacrifices. The rabbis decided that one does not apply the principle "if the day has passed, the offering lapses," because prayer is essentially a supplication for mercy. The *Tosafot* remarks that the additional prayers for the Sabbath, new moons, and festivals are not mentioned in the talmudic discussion since they are so closely tied to the sacrificial motif. With respect to the additional prayer, *musaf,* the principle "if the day has passed, the offering lapses" applies, "but all the other prayers count as 'supplications for mercy,' and 'would that a person would go on praying the whole day.'"

That the rabbis regarded supplication for mercy to be the dominant theme of the Amidah is also revealed in their opinion that the Amidah is obligatory no less for women than for men. Ordinarily, the Halakhah excuses women from all mitzvot whose performance is determined by fixed times. This might be expected to apply equally to the Shema and the Amidah, since both are recited at fixed times of the day. But the Mishnah rules that women are obligated to pray (i.e., the Amidah) (*Berakhot* 3:3). The reason given in the Jerusalem Talmud is very suggestive: "Is it not evident that in prayer each person asks for mercy for themselves?" How can we say that men will request divine mercy, but women will not? Is it not a basic need of all human beings to feel invited to stand before God in prayer? The urgent human need to supplicate for mercy overrides the technical ruling that excuses women from mitzvot performed at fixed times. The halakhic precedent of the sacrificial service in the Temple and the formal halakhic status of women with respect to mitzvot break down before the natural religious yearning of human beings for God's mercy. Prayer as yearning for mercy does not inhibit the worshiper from freely expressing "petty needs" before God.

R. Soloveitchik's understanding of prayer as self-sacrifice and as requiring justification from traditional precedents does not, however, seem to fit this rabbinic approach to prayer.

Accordingly, the Halakhah was insistent about the official character and orderliness of prayer, about the form and wording of prayer, it would be impossible to utter it. Accordingly, let us not add to it. . . . No Jew has the authority to add to the three prayers that were instituted by the scribes and sages of Israel. We do not have the authority to compose new prayers. And this is how a permanent halakhic ruling is formulated in the Talmud: "Rabbi Judah also said in the name of Samuel: 'If one was standing and saying a prayer and remembered that he had said it, he stops even in the middle'" [*Berakhot* 21a]. It is forbidden to say an obligatory prayer twice. Once is enough. One who adds is as if he had twice offered the regular sacrifice. "Rabbi ben Abba said: 'If one prays long and looks for fulfillment of his prayer, in the end he will have vexation of heart'" [*Berakhot* 32b]. We are not qualified to compose *tefillat nedavah*. Therefore, we do not now pray it. (1979b: 246)

Neither of the passages that R. Soloveitchik quotes confirms his claim that the terror of standing before God obliges us to rely totally upon precedent in order to worship. The first passage (*Berakhot* 21a) asserts that if someone begins reciting, say, the afternoon prayer and then suddenly remembers having already recited it earlier in the day, then that person must stop immediately even in the middle of a blessing. Once one has said the afternoon prayer, one's duty has been fulfilled. A repetition of the afternoon prayer can fulfill no further mitzvah. It is true that some medieval commentators raised the question, Why must the individual stop praying and not continue praying as an expression of *tefillat nedavah*? Although they ruled that this was not permissible, their ruling does not support R. Soloveitchik's notion that terror, awe, and feelings of human insignificance before God make *tefillat nedavah* impossible. Their position is based on a different principle, namely, that one may not begin with the thought of offering obligatory prayer (*tefillat hova*) and then in the middle of the Amidah decide to complete the prayer as *tefillat nedavah*. *Nedavah* and *hova* are incompatible devotional attitudes that cannot form one integrated unit of prayer.

In considering the talmudic view of free and spontaneous prayer, one should not ignore the following teaching of Rabbi Johanan.

> Rabbi Eleazar says: "If one is in doubt whether he has recited the Shema or not, he says the Shema again. If he is in doubt whether he has said the prayer [i.e., the Amidah] or not, he does not say it again." Rabbi Johanan, however, said: "Would that a man would go on praying the whole day!" (*b. Berakhot* 21a)

Why, then, was R. Soloveitchik so insistent on rejecting *tefillat nedavah* in spite of the fact that so much in the tradition supports it? In reflecting on the above criticism of R. Soloveitchik's approach to prayer, I believe that there is another way of presenting his position that would remove many of the difficulties that I raised.

TWO MODES OF STANDING IN THE PRESENCE OF GOD

I suggest that R. Soloveitchik offers two ways for individuals to experience the presence of God. One is mediated through Talmud Torah, mitzvah, and Halakhah, the other through prayer. When the focus is on learning, mitzvah or Halakhah, the covenantal Jew feels bold, creative, assertive, and fully accepted by God. Human existence is experienced as ontologically legitimate because of one's being commanded by God.

In discussing prayer, R. Soloveitchik offered an important distinction between standing in the presence of God and the halakhic formalization of prayer, which he described as being its formal technical implementation and not its true essence.

> The cosmic drama, notwithstanding its grandeur and splendor, no matter how distinctly it reflects the image of the Creator and no matter how beautifully it tells His glory, cannot provoke man to prayer. Of course, it may arouse an adoring-ecstatic mood in man; it may even inspire man to raise his voice in a song of praise and thanksgiving. Nevertheless, ecstatic adoration, even if expressed in a hymn, is not prayer. The latter transcends the bounds of liturgical worship and must not be reduced to its external-technical aspects such as praise, thanksgiving or even petition. Prayer is basically an awareness of man finding himself in the presence of and addressing himself to his Maker . . . and that the concrete performance such as the recitation of texts represents the technique of implementation of prayer and not prayer itself. (1965: 35)

R. Soloveitchik's description of the life of prayer, as distinct from his analysis of Talmud Torah, draws its inspiration from the sense of amazement and terror that accompany the religious sense of creature consciousness.

> During the recital of *Shema* man ideally feels totally committed to God and his awareness is related to a normative end, assigning to man ontological legitimacy and worth as an ethical being whom God

charged with a great mission and who is conscious of his freedom either to succeed or to fail in that mission. On the other hand, the awareness which comes with prayer is rooted in man's experiencing his "creatureliness" (to use a term coined by Rudolf Otto) and the absurdity embedded in his own existence. In contrast with the *Shema* awareness, the *Tefillah* awareness negates the legitimacy and worth of human existence. Man as a slave of God is completely dependent on Him. Man enjoys no freedom. (1965: 41 n)

When he is reflecting on the "bold adventure" of standing in the presence of God in prayer, R. Soloveitchik allows his God consciousness to be informed by sources independent of the Judaic halakhic tradition. A great deal of R. Soloveitchik's phenomenological analysis of the dialectic movements in prayer can be found in Rudolph Otto's book *The Idea of the Holy*. God consciousness, when not filtered and controlled by the normative halakhic tradition, explodes into existential antinomies and sharp dialectical movements. On one level, one desires to draw near to God, but on another level, one is repulsed and terror-stricken. R. Soloveitchik, even in his earliest writings, was vehement in his rejection of those who distorted religious life by describing it as an escape from the complex secular world to the comfort and peace of mind that prayer and the religious life offer.

That religious consciousness in man's experience which is most profound and most elevated, which penetrates to the very depths and ascends to the very heights, is not that simple and comfortable. On the contrary, it is exceptionally complex, rigorous, and tortuous. . . . It is in a condition of spiritual crisis, of psychic ascent and descent, of contradiction arising from affirmation and negation, self-abnegation and self-appreciation. . . . Religion is not, at the outset, a refuge of grace and mercy for the despondent and desperate, an enchanted stream for crushed spirits, but a raging, clamorous torrent of man's consciousness with all its crises, pangs, and torments. . . . "Out of the straits have I called, O Lord" (Ps. 118:5). "Out of the depths I have called unto Thee, O Lord" (Ps. 130:1). Out of the straits of inner oppositions and incongruities, spiritual doubts and uncertainties, out of the depths of a psyche rent with antinomies and contradictions, out of the bottomless pit of a soul that struggles with its own torments I have called, I have called unto Thee, O Lord. (1983: 141–42 n. 4)

It is only through experiencing the contradictions in human existence, through being overwhelmed by the divine presence, through the finite human being feeling terror-stricken by the infinite majesty of God that one can develop an authentic religious personality. R. Soloveitchik's criticism of modern Reform tendencies in Judaism and of the Christian Science movement is that they portray a God who offers contentment, freedom, and liberation from the tortuous ambiguities and contradictions of secular existence.

The rabbis who introduced the fixed formulas of the Amidah prayer were not simplistic legal formalists. They were fully awake to the dialectical movements felt by the terror-stricken individual who dares to stand in the presence of God. The language and structure of the Amidah educate and express the dialectical spiritual antinomies of religious life. Instead of being a straightforward behaviorist recitation, the Amidah can be understood as a rich phenomenological description of the shifting and contrary moods that express the human impossibility of prayer, on the one hand, and the gracious sense of divine love and acceptance, on the other hand.

> At the end of the Prayer we turn back to the [atmosphere of the] Blessing of the Patriarchs (Avot), the worshipper's initial approach to God. He has great confidence in the eternal God, whose mercies are unlimited, whose goodness flows from one end of the cosmos to the other. So God dwells in its midst: He is an immanent God, whose glory fills the entire world, and we know that all of reality is permeated with infinity. What is existence itself, if not the radiance of the face of the Infinite! What are riches, if not a gift of the Divine! What do we want, for what are we longing, what do we seek, if not attachment of Him and to cling to Him?! The God of Abraham, the Eternal God, who connects to the cosmos, whether from without or from within, is the God of peace and blessing and goodness. So man begins by saying: "Place peace, goodness, blessing, grace, kindness and compassion upon us and all Israel your people." That is, after all the metamorphoses and twists from love and mercy to the experience of fear and human helplessness; after the descent from the heights of longing and flight to the depths of astonishment and awe; after the nullification and seeking of the self; after the sacrifice, the Binding and ascent to the stake, and the return to reality—there once again comes the subtle experience, filled with joy and confidence: God appears to us as a sure haven and a trustworthy dwelling place. The worshipper grazes in green pastures, purifying himself before Him like a son before his father. His troubled and divided soul finds

happiness and contentment; fear is forgotten, and terror disappears. The terrible secret is past. In its place there emerge joy and the leaping toward the source of being. Man does not flee from God, but runs towards Him and clings to Him and dwells in the bosom of the Shekhinah. All is enveloped with calm and peace and quiet. The blessing of the Infinite and the kindness of the Holy One, blessed be He, flow over all, descending like dew on Mount Hermon. The world is effused with a precious light that flows from the transcendent. (1979b: 271)

Although the dialectical movement in the Amidah expresses both divine acceptance and human terror, the dominant theme that stays with the worshiper after reciting the Amidah is that of surrender and self-sacrifice.

The worshipper begins the *Amidah* prayer with the words "O Lord, open my lips, and my mouth shall speak your praises." That is, it is impossible for me to open my lips and to even say the words on my own. I stand overwhelmed before the Mighty God. Then, at the conclusion of the prayer, he takes threes steps backwards, takes leave of his Master, and falls on his face.

The institution of *Nefilat Apayim* (or *Tahanun*) is intended to emphasize man's self-abnegation. He wallows in the dust and negates his very existence. The words of supplication recited in *Nefilat Apayim* bring out the tragic coloration of the worshipper: "Be gracious to me, O Lord, for I am miserable. Heal me, O Lord, for my bones are trembling. My soul is greatly affrighted. . . . Be favorable to me with compassion and be appeased through supplication. Be favorable and appease a poor generation, for there is none to help. . . . We know not what to do, for our eyes are turned to you." All the terrors of the miserable and impoverished person, carrying within himself infinite grief and infinite disgrace, burst forth from this *Tahanun* prayer. The petitioner regrets his sins and cries out for help. The formula of petition pregnant with agony and shame is manifested in particular in the confession of sins. It is not for naught that many communities recite the *Vidui* (Confession of Sin) just before *Tahanun*. The very essence of Confession is destruction of pride and arrogance, culminating in a process of purification of the soul that raises its eyes from the depths of filth. (1979b: 263–64)

THE MAIMONIDEAN PRECEDENT

There is an important Maimonidean precedent for allowing two distinct channels to mediate the God-consciousness. If we look at Maimonides, we also discover two distinct frameworks for building the spiritual life. One derives from the halakhic normative tradition and one from the study of philosophy. Maimonides' God-awareness was deeply influenced by Aristotle and the Islamic philosophic tradition. For Maimonides, philosophical reflection on nature was not particular to the Jewish normative tradition. The God revealed in nature was available to any person willing to devote his or her life "to stand before the Lord, to serve Him, to worship Him, and to know Him."

Not only the Tribe of Levi but every single individual from among the world's inhabitants whose spirit moved him and whose intelligence gave him the understanding to withdraw from the world in order to stand before God to serve and minister to Him, to know God, and he walked upright in the manner in which God made him, shaking off from his neck the yoke of the manifold contrivances which men seek—behold, this person has been totally consecrated and God will be his portion and inheritance forever and ever. (*M. T. Laws of the Sabbatical and Jubilee Years* 13:13)

The contemplative lover of God at the end of the *Guide for the Perplexed* travels the path of philosophy in order to draw near to God. For Maimonides, if Halakhah were the only channel to mediate one's religious relationship with God, then the individual would remain—to use Maimonides' bold metaphor—outside of the palace of the king.

Those who seek to reach the ruler's habitation and to enter it, but never see the ruler's habitation, are the multitude of the adherents of the Law, I refer to the ignoramuses who observe the commandments. Those who have come up to the habitation and walk around it are the jurists who believe true opinions on the basis of traditional authority and study the law concerning the practices of divine service, but do not engage in speculation concerning the fundamental principles of religion and make no inquiry whatever regarding the rectification of belief. . . .

There are those who set their thought to work after having attained perfection in the divine science, turn

wholly toward God, may He be cherished and held sub-
lime, renounce what is other than He, and direct all
the acts of their intellect toward an examination of the
beings with a view to drawing from them proof with regard to Him, so as to know His governance of them in
whatever way it is possible. These people are those who
are present in the ruler's council. This is the rank of
the prophets. (*Guide for the Perplexed* 3:51)

The passionate love for God cannot be achieved if one's
framework of God-consciousness is exclusively mediated by Halakhah. For Maimonides, Halakhah is considered *davar katan,* a
small thing, and philosophy, physics, and metaphysics the great
thing, *davar gadol.* Although the study of Halakhah is a "small
thing," it must nevertheless be given precedence over philosophy
for the following reasons:

> For the knowledge of these things [Halakha] gives pri-
> marily composure to the mind. They are the precious
> boon bestowed by God to promote social well being
> and enable men to obtain bliss in the life hereafter.
> Moreover, the knowledge of them is within the reach of
> all, young and old, men and women; those gifted with
> great intellectual capacity as well as those whose intelli-
> gence is limited. (*M.T. Laws of the Foundations of the Torah*
> 4:13)

Maimonides never wavered in his conviction that it is only
through reflection on nature that one can become an intense lover
of God. He writes this explicitly in chapter 2 of the *Mishneh Torah,*
where he describes the path to love and awe of God.

This God, honoured and revered, it is our duty to love and fear; as it is said "Thou shalt love the Lord, thy God" (Deut. 6:5), and it is further said "Thou shalt fear the Lord, thy God" (Deut. 6:13).

And what is the way that will lead to the love of Him and the fear of Him? When a person contemplates His great and wondrous works and creatures and from them obtains a glimpse of His wisdom which is incomparable and infinite, he will straightway love Him, praise Him, glorify Him, and long with an exceeding longing to know His great Name; even as David said "My soul thirsteth for God, for the living God" (Ps. 42:3). And when he ponders these matters, he will recoil affrighted, and realize that he is a small creature, lowly and obscure, endowed with slight and slender intelligence, standing in the presence of Him who is perfect in knowledge. And so David said "When I consider Thy heavens, the work of Thy fingers—what is man that Thou art mindful of him?" (Ps. 8:4–5). (*M. T. Laws of the Foundations of the Torah* 2:1–2)

I believe that Maimonides' understanding of the halakhic and the philosophical paths to God is also operative in R. Soloveitchik's thought. The experience of prayer for Soloveitchik is similar to what philosophic contemplation was for Maimonides. The prayer experience is dominated by a theocentric passion. When dealing with Halakhah and learning, you are in an anthropocentric mode, which R. Soloveitchik describes in *Halakhic Man*. Halakhah is anthropocentric; it validates the human condition. A person's sense of self-worth before God is a central organizing principle of mitzvah. In light of the distinction between the essence of prayer—the consciousness of standing in the presence of God—and its technical halakhic structure, the worshiper senses his or her ontological insignificance before the divine presence. The contrast between *Halakhic Man* and "Ra'ayonot al ha-Tefillah" should be understood as the movement from a religious framework mediated by Torah learning and halakhic living to the world of prayer, which involves self-sacrifice, total surrender, and the felt absurdity of finite human beings attempting to stand in the presence of God.

Halakhic anthropocentrism represents one pole of R. Soloveitchik's religious anthropology. In "Ra'ayonot al ha-Tefillah" R. Soloveitchik claims that only through tragic contradictions and dichotomies does the individual grasp the depth of the theocentric dimension of prayer. R. Soloveitchik was a halakhist in the spirit of Maimonides, who allowed the theocentric passion to be nurtured by sources outside of, and sometimes in opposition to, the spirit and content of certain normative features of the halakhic tradition. Maimonides can be understood as "the redeemer of prayer" not only because of formal halakhic reasons—establishing prayer as a *mitzvah min ha-torah* (Torah sanctioned commandment)—but above all because of his having given such enormous religious weight to philosophical reflection independent of the halakhic tradition. This Maimonidean perspective can provide a precedent for R. Soloveitchik's theocentric understanding of the religious passion that should be present in the life of prayer.

This approach can also shed light on R. Soloveitchik's surprising rejection of *tefillat nedavah*. The reason given in the *Shulchan Arukh* for why one may not pray *tefillat nedavah* is because of the difficulty of sustaining *kavvanah* (concentration) throughout the entire Amidah. If, however, one could be certain of being able to sustain a devotional attitude throughout the Amidah, *tefillat nedavah* would be perfectly legitimate and acceptable.

The only plausible explanation that I can give for R. Soloveitchik's arguing so vehemently against the legitimacy of *tefillat nedavah* is that he wants prayer to communicate a God-consciousness that expresses feelings of inadequacy and terror before the divine presence. This is the religious consciousness that moved him to reject what was halakhically acceptable within the tradition and to make the bold claim that all personal prayers of petition outside of the obligatory legal framework are egoistic and express a lack of understanding of the gap that separates the human from the divine.

THE HALAKHIC AND UNIVERSAL
CONDITIONS OF THE FAITH COMMITMENT

R. Soloveitchik was a traditional talmudic master who devoted his life to teaching Talmud and to offering penetrating analyses of talmudic texts. At the same time, his religious thought was nurtured by more than one tradition. The attempt to locate him in only one tradition is a shortsighted distortion of his complex religious thought and personality. The inability to appreciate that a religious thinker may inhabit and be nurtured by distinct and often opposing religious frames of reference was also responsible for the mistaken attempt at establishing either the *Guide for the Perplexed* or the *Mishneh Torah* as the true expression of Maimonides' thinking. When you study giants of the spirit such as Maimonides or R. Soloveitchik, you witness the intellectual honesty and courage of talmudists firmly anchored in the halakhic tradition who allowed their intellectual and religious sensibilities to be influenced by frameworks of knowledge and experience independent of their particular Judaic halakhic traditions.

Those who simplify R. Soloveitchik's thought without appreciating its rich and multifaceted nature fail to do justice to the conflicting frameworks to which he was committed. His anthropocentric halakhic passion and his theocentric understanding of what it means to stand in the presence of God express the different theological traditions that nurtured his religious worldview.

Maimonides' references to Aristotle and Islamic philosophers were not motivated by pragmatic apologetic reasons but represented his sincere religious convictions and love for God. Similarly, it is deeply mistaken to assume that R. Soloveitchik's references to Western philosophers and theologians were meant to impress secular Jewish youth by dressing the halakhic tradition in sophisticated intellectual Western garb. The portrayal of R. Soloveitchik as a traditional Westernized Orthodox apologist does injustice to the authentic religious struggle reflected in his writings. It is not easy to harmonize an anthropocentric tradition mediated by mitzvah and Talmud Torah with a theocentric passion nurtured by the experiential dimensions of standing in the presence of God.

Neither for Maimonides nor for R. Soloveitchik does Halakhah control the rich and multifaceted experience of God. For Maimonides, intellectual reflection and knowledge of God in nature—the universal ground for love and awe of God—nurture a theocentric passion. For R. Soloveitchik, the universal existential features of the human condition—the terror felt by any human being yearning to stand in the presence of the Infinite—are the ground of the theocentric passion.

BIBLIOGRAPHY

The reader should note that page number citations used throughout this book for some works by Joseph B. Soloveitchik refer to the original serial publication. However, the materials are widely available in book form.

WORKS BY JOSEPH B. SOLOVEITCHIK

Soloveitchik, Joseph B. 1964. "Confrontation." *Tradition* 6, no. 2: 5–29.

———. 1965. "The Lonely Man of Faith." *Tradition* 7, no. 2: 5–67.

———. 1978a. "The Community." *Tradition* 17, no. 2: 7–24.

———. 1978b. "Majesty and Humility." *Tradition* 17, no. 2: 25–37.

———. 1978c. "Catharsis." *Tradition* 17, no. 2: 38–54.

———. 1978d. "Redemption, Prayer, Talmud Torah." *Tradition* 17, no. 2: 55–73.

———. 1979a. *Redemption.* Vol. 1 of *Reflections of the Rav.* Adapted and edited by Abraham R. Besdin. Jerusalem: Department of Torah Education and Culture in the Diaspora of the World Zionist Organization.

———. 1979b. "Ra'ayonot al ha-Tefillah." Pages 237–71 in *Ish ha-Halakhah,*

Galui v'Nistar. Jerusalem: Department for Torah Education and Culture in the Diaspora of the World Zionist Organization. Original publication: *Hadarom* 47 (1979): 84–106.

_____. 1983. *Halakhic Man.* Translated by Lawrence Kaplan. Philadelphia: Jewish Publication Society. Original publication: "Ish ha-Halakhah," *Talpioth* 1, nos. 3–4 (1944): 651–735.

_____. 1986. *The Halakhic Mind: An Essay on Jewish Tradition and Modern Thought.* Ardmore, Pa.: Seth Press; New York: Free Press.

_____. 1989. *Man of Faith in the Modern World.* Vol. 2 of *Reflections of the Rav.* Adapted and edited by Abraham R. Besdin. Hoboken, N.J.: KTAV Publishing House.

WORKS BY OTHER AUTHORS

Dorff, Elliot N. 1986. "Halakhic Man: A Review Essay." *Modern Judaism* 6, no. 1: 91–98.

Greenberg, Moshe. 1983. *Biblical Prose Prayer.* Berkeley: University of California Press.

Kaplan, Lawrence. 1988. 1984–85. "Models of the Ideal Religious Man in Rabbi Soloveitchik's Thought" (in Hebrew). *Jerusalem Studies in Jewish Thought* 4, nos. 3–4: 327–41.

Singer, David, and Moshe Sokol. 1982. "Joseph Soloveitchik: Lonely Man of Faith." *Modern Judaism* 2, no. 3: 227–72.

INDEX

A

Adam the first, 105–106,
    112–113, 118, 119, 120, 144
Adam the second, 106, 108,
    112–113, 115, 117, 118, 119,
    120, 139, 144
Akedah paradigm, 180, 181–182
A Living Covenant (Hartman),
    102
Amidah prayers, 12–13, 177,
    178–179, 180, 181, 184–186,
    197, 198–200, 203–206, 210
Animal sacrifice, 186–187
Aristotle, 30, 33, 84, 86
Assimilation and integration,
    148–149
Athens and Jerusalem, 35
Atonement, 92–94
Authenticity and individuality,
    43–44

B

Barth, 44
Buber, Martin, 128, 168

C

Confrontation. *See* Jewish
    Christian dialogue.
Covenantal faith community,
    111–119, 147–148, 149
Creation, 104–111, 118
    as *Imitatio Dei*, 81–85
    in Jewish doctrine, 86–88
    of male and female, 104–106
    and revelation, 185–186

D

Defeat and redemption, 108–111
Dorff, Elliot, 23–24, 31, 54–55
Double-confrontation model,
    143–151, 156–165

E
Ein Sof, 25
Essays
  Catharsis, 60–61
  The Community, 60
  Confrontation, 132–133, 134
  Lonely Man of Faith, 97, 100
  Prayer as Dialogue, 188
  Ra'ayonot al ha-Tefillah, 180,
    182, 185, 188, 192, 210
  Redemption, Prayer, Talmud
    Torah, 59, 178, 179–180
Ethical action, centrality of, 177

F
Faustian man, danger of, 43–46
Fear and terror, 182–187
Freedom and creativity, 95–96
Friendship, 116

G
God
  consciousness, 192–209, 212
  covenantal faith community,
    encountering, 113–116
  defeat of, 110
  divine love and intimacy,
    163–165
  encountering the lonely man of
    faith, 114
  and Israel, 11–12, 65
  man's partnership with, 81–88
  standing in the presence of,
    200–205
God in history, 9, 10–11
Greenberg, Moshe, 191–192
Guide for the Perplexed
  (Maimonides), 71–72,
  195–196, 207

H
Halakhah, 15, 23

anthropocentric, 209–210
centrality of, 154–155
and daily life, 13–14, 18
Maimonides' position on,
  206–209
mitzvot, 72, 175–176
nature of, 47–48
prayer, 175
transcendence and, 77
Halakhic man
  aesthetic sense, lack of, 30
  apologetic motif, 102
  autonomy of, 65
  Christian and Jewish sources,
    135–136
  as co-creator with God, 40–42
  cognitive man model, 31–35,
    38–39, 40
  in creation story, 104–111
  creativity, longing for, 81–85
  death, response to, 52–53,
    78–79
  Dorff critique, 23–24
  Elijah of Pruzna model for,
    50–52
  emotions and, 50–51
  evil inclination and, 54–55
  finite world and, 74–78
  freedom and autonomy of, 57,
    58, 59
  freedom and creativity, 88–91
  God's relationship to, 64–65
  and Habad Hasidic approach to
    mitzvot, 24–26
  hero, 44, 46, 47–56
  and Jewish law, 54–56, 58
  Job paradigm, 125–126
  Kantian parallel, 56–59

learning for its own sake *vs.* for practice, 36–40
legal focus of, 28–30
mathematical analogy, 32–35, 38–39, 40, 43, 47–48
mitzvot and, 24–26, 49, 64, 69–70, 76, 77, 78, 191
modernism *vs.* Talmudism, 30–33
moral activism of, 79–81
morality and divinity, 76–77
and *Musar* movement, 26–27
obedience and creativity, 40–43
philosophical *vs.* theoretical passion, 35–40
prophesy and divine providence, 155–156
and providence, 86–88
redemption and defeat, 109, 110
revelation and intellectual creativity, 64–65
self-confidence of, 68–69
self-creation and, 57, 58, 59, 95–96
sex and food, norms for, 71
sin and atonement, 92–94
theoretical study *vs.* pious action, 35–40
Torah study, 64
uniqueness of, 63–65
Vilna Gaon model for, 49–50
vs. cognitive man, 66
vs. lonely man of faith, 97–111
vs. mystical consciousness, 68
Hegel, 135
Heteronomy *vs.* autonomy, 58, 59
Homo religiousus, 66–70, 74–75, 79–81, 92–94
Human condition, three models of, 140–150

I
Identity and uniqueness, 147–148
Individuality and authenticity, 43–44
Intimacy and majesty, 119–121
I-Thou, 168

J
Jewish Christian dialogue, 131–132
Adam and Eve love analogy, 159
discussion parameters, 151–154
double-confrontation and, 160–165
human condition, three models of, 140–150
Jacob confronting Esau analogy, 157–158
love and loneliness, 139–140
mutual respect, 151
political responsum, 156–160
possibilities for, 154–156
theology and faith, 133–138

K
Kabbalistic motif of creation, 83, 84
Kant and heteronomy, 57
Kantian parallel for Halakhic man, 56–59
Kaplan, Lawrence, 99–101
Kierkegaard, 43–44, 61, 91, 135, 140

L
Leibowitz, Yeshayahu, 191
Lonely man of faith, 60, 101–104
covenantal faith community, 113, 144
in creation story, 104–111
encountering God, 114
and halakhah, 155
intimacy and majesty, 119–121

Job paradigm, 125–126
love, 139
prayer, 122–125, 168, 173,
   190
prophesy, 122
redemption, 97, 122, 139
singularity and uniqueness,
   144–145
vs. Halakhic man, 97–111
Love, 139–140, 163–165, 169

M
Maimonides, 36–37, 150, 212
   Christianity, 159–160
   God consciousness, 206–209,
      212
   Halakhah, 208–210, 212
   hero, nature of, 60–62
   miracles, 104
   philosophy of, 6
   prayer, 192–196
   providence, 87
   purity and holiness, 71–72
   teshuvah, 94
Majesty and intimacy, 119–121
Margalit, Avishai, 56, 59
Mathematical analogy, 32–35,
   38–39, 40, 43, 47–48
Mercy, supplication for, 197–198
Messianic-utopian man,
   Nachmanides, 55
Metaphysics (Aristotle), 30
Mishneh Torah (Maimonides), 83,
   94, 159–160, 192, 193, 194,
   195, 207, 208, 209
Mitzvot, 15, 24–26, 49, 64,
   69–70, 72, 76, 77, 78–81,
   175–176, 190–191
Modernism *vs.* Talmudism, 30–33
Moral autonomy, 57–58
Morality and divinity, 76–77

N
Nachmanides, 55, 192
Natural man, non-confronted
   model, 140–141
Nature, cosmic confrontation
   with, 147
Nicomachean Ethics (Aristotle), 33
Nietzsche, 43, 60, 91

O
Obedience and creativity, 40–43
Original sin, 118
Otto, Rudolph, 44, 135, 202

P
Pikuah nefesh mitzvah, 77–78
Pines, Shlomo, 6
Plato, 72
Prayer, 167, 174–175
   and *akedah* paradigm, 180,
      181–182
   Amidah, 12–13, 177, 178–179,
      180, 181, 184–186, 197,
      198–200, 203–206, 210
   animal sacrifice, 186–187
   biblical, 191–192
   community and commitment,
      176
   contemplative, 196
   and ethical action, 177
   fear and terror, 182–187
   fixed, 187–189, 193–196, 200
   gender issue, 188
   God, standing in the presence
      of, 200–205
   and God consciousness,
      192–206
   Great Assembly and, 170–171
   and Halakhah, 175
   legitimating precedent for,
      187–189

and love, 169
Maimonides' position on,
192–196
mercy, supplication for,
197–198
and mitzvot, 175–176, 191
Nachmanides' position on, 192
nedavah, 188, 195, 199–200,
210–211
patriarchs' approach, 190
petitional, 12, 124, 178
and prophesy, 122–129,
170–177, 182
in rabbinic Judaism, 11–13, 29
sacrificial motif, 196–197
Shema, 29, 201–202
spontaneous, 187, 188, 190
tehinnah vs. bakashah, 180–181
women's obligation, 198
Prophesy, 122–129, 155–156,
170–177, 182
Prophets, 88–91, 122
Providence, 86–88

R
Rabbinic Judaism
aesthetics and Greek wisdom,
15–16
attitude to Roman civilization
(Shimon Ben Yohai story),
16–18
divine power, meaning of,
10–11
eternal life *vs.* worldly activism,
16–18
mitzvah experience, 15
prayer, 11–13, 29

Reality, scientists' model for, 48
Redemption, 97, 108–111,
121–129, 139
Reform Judaism, 4, 44–45, 135
Repentance, 92–93
Revelation, 13–14, 18, 40–43,
64–65, 169
Revisionist interpretations of R.
Soloveitchik, 5–8, 19–20

S
Scheller, Max, 135
Scholem, Gershom, 76
Sin, original, 118
Sinai, terror experience, 182–183
Singer, David, 30–31, 33, 45–46,
98–99, 101, 136–137, 156
Sokol, Moshe, 30–31, 33, 45–46,
98–99, 101, 136–137, 156
Soloveitchik, Rabbi Aaron, 7
Soloveitchik, Rabbi Hayim, 24,
25, 26, 27–28, 37, 77
Spinoza, Baruch, 35
Strauss, Leo, 21

V
Vilna Gaon, 49–50

W
Western man, 120–121
Women's obligation to pray, 198

Y
Yom Kippur, 70, 77

Z
Zionism, 2, 3

Bar/Bat Mitzvah

The Bar/Bat Mitzvah Memory Book
An Album for Treasuring the Spiritual Celebration
By Rabbi Jeffrey K. Salkin and Nina Salkin

A unique album for preserving the spiritual memories of the day, and for recording plans for the Jewish future ahead. Contents include space for creating or recording family history; teachings received from rabbi, cantor, and others; mitzvot and *tzedakot* chosen and carried out, etc.
8 x 10, 48 pp, Deluxe Hardcover, 2-color text, ribbon marker, ISBN 1-58023-111-X **$19.95**

Bar/Bat Mitzvah Basics: A Practical Family Guide to Coming of Age Together
Edited by Helen Leneman. Foreword by Rabbi Jeffrey K. Salkin.
6 x 9, 240 pp, Quality PB, ISBN 1-58023-151-9 **$18.95**

For Kids—Putting God on Your Guest List: How to Claim the Spiritual Meaning
of Your Bar or Bat Mitzvah *By Rabbi Jeffrey K. Salkin*
6 x 9, 144 pp, Quality PB, ISBN 1-58023-015-6 **$14.95** *For ages 11–12*

Putting God on the Guest List: How to Reclaim the Spiritual Meaning of Your
Child's Bar or Bat Mitzvah *By Rabbi Jeffrey K. Salkin*
6 x 9, 224 pp, Quality PB, ISBN 1-879045-59-1 **$16.95**

Tough Questions Jews Ask: A Young Adult's Guide to Building a Jewish Life
By Rabbi Edward Feinstein 6 x 9, 160 pp, Quality PB, ISBN 1-58023-139-X **$14.95** *For ages 13 & up*
Also Available: **Tough Questions Jews Ask Teacher's Guide**
8½ x 11, 72 pp, PB, ISBN 1-58023-187-X **$8.95**

Bible Study/Midrash

Hineini
in Our Lives

Hineini in Our Lives: Learning How to Respond to Others through 14 Biblical Texts,
and Personal Stories *By Norman J. Cohen*
6 x 9, 240 pp, Hardcover, ISBN 1-58023-131-4 **$23.95**

Ancient Secrets: Using the Stories of the Bible to Improve Our Everyday Lives
By Rabbi Levi Meier, Ph.D. 5½ x 8½, 288 pp, Quality PB, ISBN 1-58023-064-4 **$16.95**

Moses—The Prince, the Prophet: His Life, Legend & Message for Our Lives
By Rabbi Levi Meier, Ph.D.
6 x 9, 224 pp, Quality PB, ISBN 1-58023-069-5 **$16.95**; Hardcover, ISBN 1-58023-013-X **$23.95**

Self, Struggle & Change: Family Conflict Stories in Genesis and Their Healing Insights
for Our Lives *By Norman J. Cohen* 6 x 9, 224 pp, Quality PB, ISBN 1-879045-66-4 **$16.95**

Voices from Genesis: Guiding Us through the Stages of Life *By Norman J. Cohen*
6 x 9, 192 pp, Quality PB, ISBN 1-58023-118-7 **$16.95**

Congregation Resources

Becoming a Congregation of Learners: Learning as a Key to Revitalizing
Congregational Life *By Isa Aron, Ph.D. Foreword by Rabbi Lawrence A. Hoffman.*
6 x 9, 304 pp, Quality PB, ISBN 1-58023-089-X **$19.95**

Finding a Spiritual Home: How a New Generation of Jews Can Transform the
American Synagogue *By Rabbi Sidney Schwarz*
6 x 9, 352 pp, Quality PB, ISBN 1-58023-185-3 **$19.95**

Jewish Pastoral Care: A Practical Handbook from Traditional & Contemporary Sources
Edited by Rabbi Dayle A. Friedman 6 x 9, 464 pp, Hardcover, ISBN 1-58023-078-4 **$35.00**

The Self-Renewing Congregation: Organizational Strategies for Revitalizing
Congregational Life *By Isa Aron, Ph.D. Foreword by Dr. Ron Wolfson.*
6 x 9, 304 pp, Quality PB, ISBN 1-58023-166-7 **$19.95**

Or phone, fax, mail or e-mail to: **JEWISH LIGHTS Publishing**
Sunset Farm Offices, Route 4 • P.O. Box 237 • Woodstock, Vermont 05091
Tel: (802) 457-4000 • Fax: (802) 457-4004 • www.jewishlights.com
Credit card orders: (800) 962-4544 (8:30AM–5:30PM ET Monday–Friday)
Generous discounts on quantity orders. SATISFACTION GUARANTEED. Prices subject to change.

Abraham Joshua Heschel

The Earth Is the Lord's: The Inner World of the Jew in Eastern Europe
5½ x 8, 128 pp, Quality PB, ISBN 1-879045-42-7 **$14.95**

Israel: An Echo of Eternity *New Introduction by Susannah Heschel*
5½ x 8, 272 pp, Quality PB, ISBN 1-879045-70-2 **$19.95**

A Passion for Truth: Despair and Hope in Hasidism
5½ x 8, 352 pp, Quality PB, ISBN 1-879045-41-9 **$18.99**

Holidays/Holy Days

7th Heaven: Celebrating Shabbat with Rebbe Nachman of Breslov
By Moshe Mykoff with the Breslov Research Institute
Based on the teachings of Rebbe Nachman of Breslov. Explores the art of consciously observing Shabbat and understanding in-depth many of the day's traditional spiritual practices.
5⅛ x 8¼, 224 pp, Deluxe PB w/flaps, ISBN 1-58023-175-6 **$18.95**

The Women's Passover Companion
Women's Reflections on the Festival of Freedom
Edited by Rabbi Sharon Cohen Anisfeld, Tara Mohr, and Catherine Spector
A groundbreaking collection that captures the voices of Jewish women who engage in a provocative conversation about women's relationships to Passover as well as the roots and meanings of women's seders.
6 x 9, 352 pp, Hardcover, ISBN 1-58023-128-4 **$24.95**

The Women's Seder Sourcebook
Rituals & Readings for Use at the Passover Seder
Edited by Rabbi Sharon Cohen Anisfeld, Tara Mohr, and Catherine Spector
This practical guide gathers the voices of more than one hundred women in readings, personal and creative reflections, commentaries, blessings, and ritual suggestions that can be incorporated into your Passover celebration as supplements to or substitutes for traditional passages of the haggadah.
6 x 9, 384 pp, Hardcover, ISBN 1-58023-136-5 **$24.95**

Creating Lively Passover Seders: A Sourcebook of Engaging Tales, Texts & Activities
By David Arnow, Ph.D.
7 x 9, 416 pp, Quality PB, ISBN 1-58023-184-5 **$24.99**

Hanukkah, 2nd Edition: The Family Guide to Spiritual Celebration
By Dr. Ron Wolfson. Edited by Joel Lurie Grishaver.
7 x 9, 240 pp, illus., Quality PB, ISBN 1-58023-122-5 **$18.95**

The Jewish Family Fun Book: Holiday Projects, Everyday Activities, and Travel Ideas
with Jewish Themes *By Danielle Dardashti and Roni Sarig. Illus. by Avi Katz.*
6 x 9, 288 pp, 70+ b/w illus. & diagrams, Quality PB, ISBN 1-58023-171-3 **$18.95**

The Jewish Gardening Cookbook: Growing Plants & Cooking for
Holidays & Festivals *By Michael Brown*
6 x 9, 224 pp, 30+ illus., Quality PB, ISBN 1-58023-116-0 **$16.95**;
Hardcover, ISBN 1-58023-004-0 **$21.95**

Passover, 2nd Edition: The Family Guide to Spiritual Celebration
By Dr. Ron Wolfson with Joel Lurie Grishaver
7 x 9, 352 pp, Quality PB, ISBN 1-58023-174-8 **$19.95**

Shabbat, 2nd Edition: The Family Guide to Preparing for and Celebrating the Sabbath
By Dr. Ron Wolfson 7 x 9, 320 pp, illus., Quality PB, ISBN 1-58023-164-0 **$19.95**

Sharing Blessings: Children's Stories for Exploring the Spirit of the Jewish Holidays
By Rahel Musleah and Michael Klayman
8½ x 11, 64 pp, Full-color illus., Hardcover, ISBN 1-879045-71-0 **$18.95** *For ages 6 & up*

Inspiration

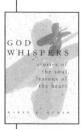

God in All Moments
Mystical & Practical Spiritual Wisdom from Hasidic Masters
Edited and translated by Or N. Rose with Ebn D. Leader
Hasidic teachings on how to be mindful in religious practice and how to cultivate everyday ethical behavior—*hanhagot.* 5½ x 8½, 192 pp, Quality PB, ISBN 1-58023-186-1 **$16.95**

Our Dance with God: Finding Prayer, Perspective and Meaning in the Stories of Our Lives *By Karyn D. Kedar* 6 x 9, 176 pp, Quality PB, ISBN 1-58023-202-7 **$16.99**

Also Available: **The Dance of the Dolphin** (Hardcover edition of *Our Dance with God*)
6 x 9, 176 pp, Hardcover, ISBN 1-58023-154-3 **$19.95**

The Empty Chair: Finding Hope and Joy—Timeless Wisdom from a Hasidic Master, Rebbe Nachman of Breslov *Adapted by Moshe Mykoff and the Breslov Research Institute*
4 x 6, 128 pp, 2-color text, Deluxe PB w/flaps, ISBN 1-879045-67-2 **$9.95**

The Gentle Weapon: Prayers for Everyday and Not-So-Everyday Moments— Timeless Wisdom from the Teachings of the Hasidic Master, Rebbe Nachman of Breslov *Adapted by Moshe Mykoff and S. C. Mizrahi, together with the Breslov Research Institute*
4 x 6, 144 pp, 2-color text, Deluxe PB w/flaps, ISBN 1-58023-022-9 **$9.95**

God Whispers: Stories of the Soul, Lessons of the Heart *By Karyn D. Kedar*
6 x 9, 176 pp, Quality PB, ISBN 1-58023-088-1 **$15.95**

An Orphan in History: One Man's Triumphant Search for His Jewish Roots
By Paul Cowan. Afterword by Rachel Cowan. 6 x 9, 288 pp, Quality PB, ISBN 1-58023-135-7 **$16.95**

Restful Reflections: Nighttime Inspiration to Calm the Soul, Based on Jewish Wisdom *By Rabbi Kerry M. Olitzky & Rabbi Lori Forman*
4½ x 6½, 448 pp, Quality PB, ISBN 1-58023-091-1 **$15.95**

Sacred Intentions: Daily Inspiration to Strengthen the Spirit, Based on Jewish Wisdom *By Rabbi Kerry M. Olitzky and Rabbi Lori Forman*
4½ x 6½, 448 pp, Quality PB, ISBN 1-58023-061-X **$15.95**

Kabbalah/Mysticism/Enneagram

Seek My Face: A Jewish Mystical Theology
By Dr. Arthur Green
This classic work of contemporary Jewish theology, revised and updated, is a profound, deeply personal statement of the lasting truths of Jewish mysticism and the basic faith claims of Judaism. A tool for anyone seeking the elusive presence of God in the world. 6 x 9, 304 pp, Quality PB, ISBN 1-58023-130-6 **$19.95**

Zohar: Annotated & Explained
Translation and annotation by Dr. Daniel C. Matt. Foreword by Andrew Harvey, SkyLight Illuminations series editor.
Offers insightful yet unobtrusive commentary to the masterpiece of Jewish mysticism that explains references and mystical symbols, shares wisdom of spiritual masters, and clarifies the *Zohar*'s bold claim: We have always been taught that we need God, but in order to manifest in the world, God needs us.
5½ x 8½, 160 pp, Quality PB, ISBN 1-893361-51-9 **$15.99** (A SkyLight Paths book)

Cast in God's Image: Discover Your Personality Type Using the Enneagram and Kabbalah *By Rabbi Howard A. Addison*
7 x 9, 176 pp, Quality PB, Layflat binding, 20+ journaling exercises, ISBN 1-58023-124-1 **$16.95**

Ehyeh: A Kabbalah for Tomorrow *By Dr. Arthur Green*
6 x 9, 224 pp, Hardcover, ISBN 1-58023-125-X **$21.99**

The Enneagram and Kabbalah: Reading Your Soul *By Rabbi Howard A. Addison*
6 x 9, 176 pp, Quality PB, ISBN 1-58023-001-6 **$15.95**

Finding Joy: A Practical Spiritual Guide to Happiness *By Dannel I. Schwartz with Mark Hass*
6 x 9, 192 pp, Quality PB, ISBN 1-58023-009-1 **$14.95**; Hardcover, ISBN 1-879045-53-2 **$19.95**

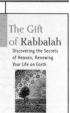

The Gift of Kabbalah: Discovering the Secrets of Heaven, Renewing Your Life on Earth *By Tamar Frankiel, Ph.D.*
6 x 9, 256 pp, Quality PB, ISBN 1-58023-141-1 **$16.95**; Hardcover, ISBN 1-58023-108-X **$21.95**

The Way Into Jewish Mystical Tradition *By Lawrence Kushner*
6 x 9, 224 pp, Quality PB, ISBN 1-58023-200-0 **$18.99**; Hardcover, ISBN 1-58023-029-6 **$21.95**

Spirituality

The Alphabet of Paradise: An A–Z of Spirituality for Everyday Life
By Rabbi Howard Cooper
In twenty-six engaging chapters, Cooper spiritually illuminates the subjects of our daily lives—A to Z—examining these sources by using an ancient Jewish mystical method of interpretation that reveals both the literal and more allusive meanings of each.   5 x 7¾, 224 pp, Quality PB, ISBN 1-893361-80-2 **$16.95** *(A SkyLight Paths book)*

Does the Soul Survive?: A Jewish Journey to Belief in Afterlife, Past Lives & Living with Purpose   *By Rabbi Elie Kaplan Spitz. Foreword by Brian L. Weiss, M.D.*
Spitz relates his own experiences and those shared with him by people he has worked with as a rabbi, and shows us that belief in afterlife and past lives, so often approached with reluctance, is in fact true to Jewish tradition.
6 x 9, 288 pp, Quality PB, ISBN 1-58023-165-9 **$16.99**; Hardcover, ISBN 1-58023-094-6 **$21.95**

First Steps to a New Jewish Spirit: Reb Zalman's Guide to Recapturing the Intimacy & Ecstasy in Your Relationship with God
By Rabbi Zalman M. Schachter-Shalomi with Donald Gropman
An extraordinary spiritual handbook that restores psychic and physical vigor by introducing us to new models and alternative ways of practicing Judaism. Offers meditation and contemplation exercises for enriching the most important aspects of everyday life.   6 x 9, 144 pp, Quality PB, ISBN 1-58023-182-9 **$16.95**

God in Our Relationships: Spirituality between People from the Teachings of Martin Buber   *By Rabbi Dennis S. Ross*
On the eightieth anniversary of Buber's classic work, we can discover new answers to critical issues in our lives. Inspiring examples from Ross's own life— as congregational rabbi, father, hospital chaplain, social worker, and husband— illustrate Buber's difficult-to-understand ideas about how we encounter God and each other. 5½ x 8½, 160 pp, Quality PB, ISBN 1-58023-147-0 **$16.95**

The Jewish Lights Spirituality Handbook: A Guide to Understanding, Exploring & Living a Spiritual Life   *Edited by Stuart M. Matlins*
What exactly is "Jewish" about spirituality? How do I make it a part of my life? Fifty of today's foremost spiritual leaders share their ideas and experience with us.
6 x 9, 456 pp, Quality PB, ISBN 1-58023-093-8 **$19.99**; Hardcover, ISBN 1-58023-100-4 **$24.95**

Bringing the Psalms to Life: How to Understand and Use the Book of Psalms
By Dr. Daniel F. Polish
6 x 9, 208 pp, Quality PB, ISBN 1-58023-157-8 **$16.95**; Hardcover, ISBN 1-58023-077-6 **$21.95**

God & the Big Bang: Discovering Harmony between Science & Spirituality
By Dr. Daniel C. Matt   6 x 9, 216 pp, Quality PB, ISBN 1-879045-89-3 **$16.95**

Godwrestling—Round 2: Ancient Wisdom, Future Paths
By Rabbi Arthur Waskow   6 x 9, 352 pp, Quality PB, ISBN 1-879045-72-9 **$18.95**

One God Clapping: The Spiritual Path of a Zen Rabbi   *By Rabbi Alan Lew with Sherril Jaffe*
5½ x 8½, 336 pp, Quality PB, ISBN 1-58023-115-2 **$16.95**

The Path of Blessing: Experiencing the Energy and Abundance of the Divine
By Rabbi Marcia Prager   5½ x 8½, 240 pp., Quality PB, ISBN 1-58023-148-9 **$16.95**

Six Jewish Spiritual Paths: A Rationalist Looks at Spirituality   *By Rabbi Rifat Sonsino*
6 x 9, 208 pp, Quality PB, ISBN 1-58023-167-5 **$16.95**; Hardcover, ISBN 1-58023-095-4 **$21.95**

Soul Judaism: Dancing with God into a New Era
By Rabbi Wayne Dosick   5½ x 8½, 304 pp, Quality PB, ISBN 1-58023-053-9 **$16.95**

Stepping Stones to Jewish Spiritual Living: Walking the Path Morning, Noon, and Night   *By Rabbi James L. Mirel and Karen Bonnell Werth*
6 x 9, 240 pp, Quality PB, ISBN 1-58023-074-1 **$16.95**; Hardcover, ISBN 1-58023-003-2 **$21.95**

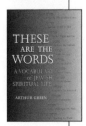

There Is No Messiah... and You're It: The Stunning Transformation of Judaism's Most Provocative Idea   *By Rabbi Robert N. Levine, D.D.*
6 x 9, 192 pp, Hardcover, ISBN 1-58023-173-X **$21.95**

These Are the Words: A Vocabulary of Jewish Spiritual Life   *By Dr. Arthur Green*
6 x 9, 304 pp, Quality PB, ISBN 1-58023-107-1 **$18.95**

Spirituality/Lawrence Kushner

The Book of Letters: A Mystical Hebrew Alphabet
Popular Hardcover Edition, 6 x 9, 80 pp, 2-color text, ISBN 1-879045-00-1 **$24.95**
Deluxe Gift Edition with slipcase, 9 x 12, 80 pp, 4-color text, Hardcover, ISBN 1-879045-01-X **$79.95**
Collector's Limited Edition, 9 x 12, 80 pp, gold foil embossed pages, w/limited edition silkscreened
print, ISBN 1-879045-04-4 **$349.00**

The Book of Miracles: A Young Person's Guide to Jewish Spiritual Awareness
All-new illustrations by the author
6 x 9, 96 pp, 2-color illus., Hardcover, ISBN 1-879045-78-8 **$16.95** *For ages 9–13*

The Book of Words: Talking Spiritual Life, Living Spiritual Talk
6 x 9, 160 pp, Quality PB, ISBN 1-58023-020-2 **$16.95**

Eyes Remade for Wonder: A Lawrence Kushner Reader
Introduction by Thomas Moore
6 x 9, 240 pp, Quality PB, ISBN 1-58023-042-3 **$18.95;** Hardcover, ISBN 1-58023-014-8 **$23.95**

God Was in This Place & I, i Did Not Know
Finding Self, Spirituality and Ultimate Meaning
6 x 9, 192 pp, Quality PB, ISBN 1-879045-33-8 **$16.95**

Honey from the Rock: An Introduction to Jewish Mysticism
6 x 9, 176 pp, Quality PB, ISBN 1-58023-073-3 **$16.95**

Invisible Lines of Connection: Sacred Stories of the Ordinary
5½ x 8½, 160 pp, Quality PB, ISBN 1-879045-98-2 **$15.95**

Jewish Spirituality—A Brief Introduction for Christians
5½ x 8½, 112 pp, Quality PB Original, ISBN 1-58023-150-0 **$12.95**

The River of Light: Jewish Mystical Awareness
6 x 9, 192 pp, Quality PB, ISBN 1-58023-096-2 **$16.95**

The Way Into Jewish Mystical Tradition
6 x 9, 224 pp, Quality PB, ISBN 1-58023-200-0 **$18.99;** Hardcover, ISBN 1-58023-029-6 **$21.95**

Spirituality/Prayer

Pray Tell: A Hadassah Guide to Jewish Prayer
By Rabbi Jules Harlow, with contributions from Tamara Cohen, Rochelle Furstenberg, Rabbi Daniel Gordis, Leora Tanenbaum, and many others
A guide to traditional Jewish prayer enriched with insight and wisdom from a broad variety of viewpoints—from Orthodox, Conservative, Reform, and Reconstructionist Judaism to New Age and feminist. Offers fresh and modern slants on what it means to pray as a Jew, and how women and men might actually pray. 8½ x 11, 400 pp, Quality PB, ISBN 1-58023-163-2 **$29.95**

My People's Prayer Book Series
Traditional Prayers, Modern Commentaries
Edited by Rabbi Lawrence A. Hoffman
Provides diverse and exciting commentary to the traditional liturgy, helping modern men and women find new wisdom in Jewish prayer, and bring liturgy into their lives.

Each book includes Hebrew text, modern translation, and commentaries from all perspectives of the Jewish world.
Vol. 1—The *Sh'ma* and Its Blessings
7 x 10, 168 pp, Hardcover, ISBN 1-879045-79-6 **$23.95**
Vol. 2—The *Amidah*
7 x 10, 240 pp, Hardcover, ISBN 1-879045-80-X **$24.95**
Vol. 3—*P'sukei D'zimrah* (Morning Psalms)
7 x 10, 240 pp, Hardcover, ISBN 1-879045-81-8 **$24.95**
Vol. 4—*Seder K'riat Hatorah* (The Torah Service)
7 x 10, 264 pp, Hardcover, ISBN 1-879045-82-6 **$23.95**
Vol. 5—*Birkhot Hashachar* (Morning Blessings)
7 x 10, 240 pp, Hardcover, ISBN 1-879045-83-4 **$24.95**
Vol. 6—*Tachanun* and Concluding Prayers
7 x 10, 240 pp, Hardcover, ISBN 1-879045-84-2 **$24.95**
Vol. 7—Shabbat at Home
7 x 10, 240 pp, Hardcover, ISBN 1-879045-85-0 **$24.95**

Spirituality/The Way Into... Series

The Way Into... Series offers an accessible and highly usable "guided tour" of the Jewish faith, people, history and beliefs—in total, an introduction to Judaism that will enable you to understand and interact with the sacred texts of the Jewish tradition. Each volume is written by a leading contemporary scholar and teacher, and explores one key aspect of Judaism. *The Way Into...* enables all readers to achieve a real sense of Jewish cultural literacy through guided study.

The Way Into Encountering God in Judaism   *By Neil Gillman*
6 x 9, 240 pp, Quality PB, ISBN 1-58023-199-3 **$18.99**; Hardcover, ISBN 1-58023-025-3 **$21.95**

Also Available: **The Jewish Approach to God: A Brief Introduction for Christians**
By Neil Gillman 5½ x 8½, 192 pp, Quality PB, ISBN 1-58023-190-X **$16.95**

The Way Into Jewish Mystical Tradition   *By Lawrence Kushner*
6 x 9, 224 pp, Quality PB, ISBN 1-58023-200-0 **$18.99**; Hardcover, ISBN 1-58023-029-6 **$21.95**

The Way Into Jewish Prayer   *By Lawrence A. Hoffman*
6 x 9, 224 pp, Quality PB, ISBN 1-58023-201-9 **$18.99**; Hardcover, ISBN 1-58023-027-X **$21.95**

The Way Into Torah   *By Norman J. Cohen*
6 x 9, 176 pp, Quality PB, ISBN 1-58023-198-5 **$16.99**; Hardcover, ISBN 1-58023-028-8 **$21.95**

Spirituality in the Workplace

Being God's Partner
How to Find the Hidden Link Between Spirituality and Your Work
By Rabbi Jeffrey K. Salkin. Introduction by Norman Lear.
6 x 9, 192 pp, Quality PB, ISBN 1-879045-65-6 **$17.95**

The Business Bible: 10 New Commandments for Bringing Spirituality & Ethical Values into the Workplace   *By Rabbi Wayne Dosick*
5½ x 8½, 208 pp, Quality PB, ISBN 1-58023-101-2 **$14.95**

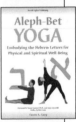

Spirituality and Wellness

Aleph-Bet Yoga
Embodying the Hebrew Letters for Physical and Spiritual Well-Being
By Steven A. Rapp. Foreword by Tamar Frankiel, Ph.D., and Judy Greenfeld. Preface by Hart Lazer
7 x 10, 128 pp, b/w photos, Quality PB, Layflat binding, ISBN 1-58023-162-4 **$16.95**

Entering the Temple of Dreams
Jewish Prayers, Movements, and Meditations for the End of the Day
By Tamar Frankiel, Ph.D., and Judy Greenfeld
7 x 10, 192 pp, illus., Quality PB, ISBN 1-58023-079-2 **$16.95**

Minding the Temple of the Soul
Balancing Body, Mind, and Spirit through Traditional Jewish Prayer, Movement, and Meditation   *By Tamar Frankiel, Ph.D., and Judy Greenfeld*
7 x 10, 184 pp, illus., Quality PB, ISBN 1-879045-64-8 **$16.95**
Audiotape of the Blessings and Meditations: 60 min. **$9.95**
Videotape of the Movements and Meditations: 46 min. **$20.00**

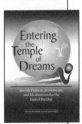

Spirituality/Women's Interest

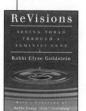

Lifecycles, Vol. 1: Jewish Women on Life Passages & Personal Milestones
Edited and with introductions by Rabbi Debra Orenstein
6 x 9, 480 pp, Quality PB, ISBN 1-58023-018-0 **$19.95**

Lifecycles, Vol. 2: Jewish Women on Biblical Themes in Contemporary Life
Edited and with introductions by Rabbi Debra Orenstein and Rabbi Jane Rachel Litman
6 x 9, 464 pp, Quality PB, ISBN 1-58023-019-9 **$19.95**

Moonbeams: A Hadassah Rosh Hodesh Guide *Edited by Carol Diament, Ph.D.*
8½ x 11, 240 pp, Quality PB, ISBN 1-58023-099-7 **$20.00**

ReVisions: Seeing Torah through a Feminist Lens *By Rabbi Elyse Goldstein*
5½ x 8½, 224 pp, Quality PB, ISBN 1-58023-117-9 **$16.95**

White Fire: A Portrait of Women Spiritual Leaders in America
By Rabbi Malka Drucker. Photographs by Gay Block.
7 x 10, 320 pp, 30+ b/w photos, Hardcover, ISBN 1-893361-64-0 **$24.95** *(A SkyLight Paths book)*

Women of the Wall: Claiming Sacred Ground at Judaism's Holy Site
Edited by Phyllis Chesler and Rivka Haut
6 x 9, 496 pp, b/w photos, Hardcover, ISBN 1-58023-161-6 **$34.95**

The Women's Haftarah Commentary: New Insights from Women Rabbis on
the 54 Weekly Haftarah Portions, the 5 Megillot & Special Shabbatot
Edited by Rabbi Elyse Goldstein   6 x 9, 560 pp, Hardcover, ISBN 1-58023-133-0 **$39.99**

The Women's Torah Commentary: New Insights from Women Rabbis on the 54
Weekly Torah Portions   *Edited by Rabbi Elyse Goldstein*
6 x 9, 496 pp, Hardcover, ISBN 1-58023-076-8 **$34.95**

The Year Mom Got Religion: One Woman's Midlife Journey into Judaism
By Lee Meyerhoff Hendler
6 x 9, 208 pp, Quality PB, ISBN 1-58023-070-9 **$15.95**; Hardcover, ISBN 1-58023-000-8 **$19.95**

See Holidays for *The Women's Passover Companion: Women's Reflections on the Festival of Freedom* and *The Women's Seder Sourcebook: Rituals & Readings for Use at the Passover Seder.*

Travel

Israel—A Spiritual Travel Guide: A Companion for the Modern Jewish Pilgrim
By Rabbi Lawrence A. Hoffman   4¾ x 10, 256 pp, Quality PB, illus., ISBN 1-879045-56-7 **$18.95**
Also Available: **The Israel Mission Leader's Guide**   ISBN 1-58023-085-7 **$4.95**

12 Steps

100 Blessings Every Day
Daily Twelve Step Recovery Affirmations, Exercises for Personal Growth &
Renewal Reflecting Seasons of the Jewish Year
By Rabbi Kerry M. Olitzky. Foreword by Rabbi Neil Gillman.
Using a one-day-at-a-time monthly format, this guide reflects on the rhythm of
the Jewish calendar to help bring insight to recovery from addictions and com-
pulsive behaviors of all kinds. Its exercises help us move from *thinking* to *doing.*
4½ x 6½, 432 pp, Quality PB, ISBN 1-879045-30-3 **$15.99**

Recovery from Codependence: A Jewish Twelve Steps Guide to Healing Your Soul
By Rabbi Kerry M. Olitzky   6 x 9, 160 pp, Quality PB, ISBN 1-879045-32-X **$13.95**

Renewed Each Day: Daily Twelve Step Recovery Meditations Based on the Bible
By Rabbi Kerry M. Olitzky and Aaron Z.
Vol. 1—Genesis & Exodus:
6 x 9, 224 pp, Quality PB, ISBN 1-879045-12-5 **$14.95**
Vol. 2—Leviticus, Numbers & Deuteronomy:
6 x 9, 280 pp, Quality PB, ISBN 1-879045-13-3 **$14.95**

Twelve Jewish Steps to Recovery
A Personal Guide to Turning from Alcoholism & Other Addictions—Drugs, Food,
Gambling, Sex...
By Rabbi Kerry M. Olitzky and Stuart A. Copans, M.D. Preface by Abraham J. Twerski, M.D.
6 x 9, 144 pp, Quality PB, ISBN 1-879045-09-5 **$14.95**

Theology/Philosophy

Aspects of Rabbinic Theology
By Solomon Schechter. New Introduction by Dr. Neil Gillman.
6 x 9, 448 pp, Quality PB, ISBN 1-879045-24-9 **$19.95**

Broken Tablets: Restoring the Ten Commandments and Ourselves
Edited by Rachel S. Mikva. Introduction by Lawrence Kushner. Afterword by Arnold Jacob Wolf.
6 x 9, 192 pp, Quality PB, ISBN 1-58023-158-6 **$16.95**; Hardcover, ISBN 1-58023-066-0 **$21.95**

Creating an Ethical Jewish Life
A Practical Introduction to Classic Teachings on How to Be a Jew
By Dr. Byron L. Sherwin and Seymour J. Cohen
6 x 9, 336 pp, Quality PB, ISBN 1-58023-114-4 **$19.95**

The Death of Death: Resurrection and Immortality in Jewish Thought
By Dr. Neil Gillman 6 x 9, 336 pp, Quality PB, ISBN 1-58023-081-4 **$18.95**

Evolving Halakhah: A Progressive Approach to Traditional Jewish Law
By Rabbi Dr. Moshe Zemer
6 x 9, 480 pp, Quality PB, ISBN 1-58023-127-6 **$29.95**; Hardcover, ISBN 1-58023-002-4 **$40.00**

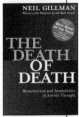

Hasidic Tales: Annotated & Explained
By Rabbi Rami Shapiro. Foreword by Andrew Harvey, SkyLight Illuminations series editor.
5½ x 8½, 240 pp, Quality PB, ISBN 1-893361-86-1 **$16.95** *(A SkyLight Paths Book)*

A Heart of Many Rooms: Celebrating the Many Voices within Judaism
By Dr. David Hartman
6 x 9, 352 pp, Quality PB, ISBN 1-58023-156-X **$19.95**; Hardcover, ISBN 1-58023-048-2 **$24.95**

Judaism and Modern Man: An Interpretation of Jewish Religion
By Will Herberg. New Introduction by Dr. Neil Gillman.
5½ x 8½, 336 pp, Quality PB, ISBN 1-879045-87-7 **$18.95**

Keeping Faith with the Psalms: Deepen Your Relationship with God Using the
Book of Psalms *By Daniel F. Polish*
6 x 9, 272 pp, Hardcover, ISBN 1-58023-179-9 **$24.95**

The Last Trial
On the Legends and Lore of the Command to Abraham to Offer Isaac as a Sacrifice
By Shalom Spiegel. New Introduction by Judah Goldin.
6 x 9, 208 pp, Quality PB, ISBN 1-879045-29-X **$18.95**

A Living Covenant: The Innovative Spirit in Traditional Judaism
By Dr. David Hartman 6 x 9, 368 pp, Quality PB, ISBN 1-58023-011-3 **$18.95**

Love and Terror in the God Encounter
The Theological Legacy of Rabbi Joseph B. Soloveitchik
By Dr. David Hartman
6 x 9, 240 pp, Quality PB, ISBN 1-58023-176-4 **$19.95**; Hardcover, ISBN 1-58023-112-8 **$25.00**

Seeking the Path to Life
Theological Meditations on God and the Nature of People, Love, Life and Death
By Rabbi Ira F. Stone 6 x 9, 160 pp, Quality PB, ISBN 1-879045-47-8 **$14.95**

The Spirit of Renewal: Finding Faith after the Holocaust
By Rabbi Edward Feld 6 x 9, 224 pp, Quality PB, ISBN 1-879045-40-0 **$16.95**

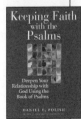

Tormented Master: *The Life and Spiritual Quest of Rabbi Nahman of Bratslav*
By Dr. Arthur Green 6 x 9, 416 pp, Quality PB, ISBN 1-879045-11-7 **$19.99**

Your Word Is Fire: The Hasidic Masters on Contemplative Prayer
Edited and translated by Dr. Arthur Green and Barry W. Holtz
6 x 9, 160 pp, Quality PB, ISBN 1-879045-25-7 **$15.95**

I Am Jewish
Personal Reflections Inspired by the Last Words of Daniel Pearl
Almost 150 Jews—both famous and not—from all walks of life, from all around
the world, write about Identity, Heritage, Covenant/Chosenness and Faith,
Humanity and Ethnicity, and *Tikkun Olam* and Justice.
Edited by Judea and Ruth Pearl
6 x 9, 304 pp, Hardcover, ISBN 1-58023-183-7 **$24.99**

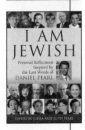

About Jewish Lights

People of all faiths and backgrounds yearn for books that attract, engage, educate, and spiritually inspire.

Our principal goal is to stimulate thought and help all people learn about who the Jewish People are, where they come from, and what the future can be made to hold. While people of our diverse Jewish heritage are the primary audience, our books speak to people in the Christian world as well and will broaden their understanding of Judaism and the roots of their own faith.

We bring to you authors who are at the forefront of spiritual thought and experience. While each has something different to say, they all say it in a voice that you can hear.

Our books are designed to welcome you and then to engage, stimulate, and inspire. We judge our success not only by whether or not our books are beautiful and commercially successful, but by whether or not they make a difference in your life.

For your information and convenience, at the back of this book we have provided a list of other Jewish Lights books you might find interesting and useful. They cover all the categories of your life:

Bar/Bat Mitzvah	Life Cycle
Bible Study / Midrash	Meditation
Children's Books	Parenting
Congregation Resources	Prayer
Current Events / History	Ritual / Sacred Practice
Ecology	Spirituality
Fiction: Mystery, Science Fiction	Theology / Philosophy
Grief / Healing	Travel
Holidays / Holy Days	Twelve Steps
Inspiration	Women's Interest
Kabbalah / Mysticism / Enneagram	

Stuart M. Matlins, Publisher

Or phone, fax, mail or e-mail to: **JEWISH LIGHTS Publishing**
Sunset Farm Offices, Route 4 • P.O. Box 237 • Woodstock, Vermont 05091
Tel: (802) 457-4000 • Fax: (802) 457-4004 • www.jewishlights.com
Credit card orders: **(800) 962-4544** (8:30AM–5:30PM ET Monday–Friday)
Generous discounts on quantity orders. SATISFACTION GUARANTEED. Prices subject to change.

For more information about each book, visit our website at www.jewishlights.com